CATHOLIC AND FRANCISCAN ETHICS

THE ESSENTIALS

First Edition

By John Mizzoni
Neumann University

cognella®
academic publishing

Nihil obstat: Robert A. Pesarchick
Imprimatur: Archbishop Charles J. Chaput, OFM, Cap.
Archdiocese of Philadelphia
July 19, 2013

Bassim Hamadeh, CEO and Publisher
Michael Simpson, Vice President of Acquisitions
Jamie Giganti, Managing Editor
Jess Busch, Senior Graphic Designer
John Remington, Acquisitions Editor
Brian Fahey, Licensing Specialist
Kaela Martin, Interior Designer

Printed in the United States of America

ISBN: 978-1-63189-528-9 (pbk) / 978-1-63189-529-6 (br)

www.cognella.com   800-200-3908

CONTENTS

ACKNOWLEDGMENTS

T his book would not be possible without the assistance of Phil Pegan, Vince Riley, and Geoff Karabin, three of my colleagues at Neumann University. Through many discussions over the course of several years, they helped me think through the material and helped me organize it.

For many years this book was only an idea for us. And it is only through the support of Neumann University in granting me a course release in the fall 2011 semester that I was able to begin to turn the idea into a manuscript. I am grateful for the support of Neumann University, particularly Gerry O'Sullivan, and Mac Given, in helping me to finally get this project off the ground.

I must also extend my thanks to Sister Patricia Hutchison, who directs the Neumann Institute for Franciscan Studies at Neumann University. Sister Pat has supplied me with innumerable Catholic and Franciscan materials over the years, and has given me valuable direction and encouragement.

Most importantly, I must thank the students of Philosophy 102 (Exploring Ethics) who assisted me by reading through and commenting on initial drafts of some of the chapters. This book was written for my ethics students, particularly the ones who would often comment about the book on Catholic ethics that we were using at the time (fall 2010), that "it was difficult to read" and "very difficult to understand especially without having a religious background."

It is my intention that *Catholic and Franciscan Ethics: The Essentials* can be understandable and helpful to all readers, regardless of their background.

INTRODUCTION

The Catholic and Franciscan ethical traditions offer an ethical framework with many dimensions. This book seeks to spell out those dimensions for those who are unfamiliar with these traditions.

Why This Book?

This book is an introduction to the essentials of the Catholic and Franciscan ethical traditions. It is meant as a supplement to be used in conjunction with other materials. Other books and authors that can be consulted in order to go into more depth with these two ethical traditions are provided throughout the text and in several appendices.

The Catholic tradition and the Franciscan tradition are two different traditions that are historically entangled and intertwined. In order to provide a clear introduction to both traditions, I have treated the Catholic ethical tradition in the early chapters of the book and the Franciscan ethical tradition in the later chapters of the book. Some readers may only be interested in a brief introduction to the Catholic ethical tradition, and so they would be most interested in chapters 1 through 4. Thus, this brief supplement can be of use for non-Franciscans.

Other readers who are interested in the Franciscan ethical tradition will not only want to read chapters 5 and 6, which specifically focus on the Franciscan tradition, but will also be interested in reading the first four chapters of the book because the Franciscan ethical tradition grows out of and then contributes to the Catholic ethical tradition.

Stylistically, the book is written in a way that makes it very accessible to a wide audience. I do not assume that the reader has a Catholic or Franciscan background. I regard the text as genuinely introductory. Not only is the writing style very accessible, but the text incorporates features designed to aid reader understanding, such as diagrams, key concepts gathered together at the end of each chapter, review and discussion questions about each chapter, call-outs in various chapters, as well as several appendices that consist of a glossary, a summary of all key concepts, and recommended additional readings.

Yet even those readers who are familiar with the Catholic and Franciscan traditions may find the book valuable because it provides a short, quick, elementary introduction that concisely gathers together all of the main components of the Catholic and Franciscan ethical traditions. So instead of being thought of as an introduction, the book can also be thought of as a refresher of the essentials of these two ethical traditions.

The Catholic Tradition

As an initial step toward understanding the rich ethical framework of the Catholic and Franciscan traditions, we will first consider the Catholic tradition by itself, along a time line, one that is relevant to the study of ethics.

The Catholic tradition has ancient roots, and these roots extend all the way back to the Bible. The oldest parts of the Bible, the Old Testament (made up of forty-six books), were written roughly one thousand years before the time of Jesus. The New Testament of the Bible (made up of twenty-seven books), which contains the life and teachings of Jesus, was also written in ancient times (roughly between the years 50 to 150 CE).

Jesus lived during the time of the ancient Roman Empire. Chapter 1 of *Catholic and Franciscan Ethics (CFE)* focuses on ancient Catholic ethics and looks at important ethical concepts and principles that appear in the Bible. From the Old Testament of the Bible, for instance, we will look at the Ten Commandments. From the New Testament of the Bible we will look at the Gospels, which are the books of the Bible that describe the words and actions of Jesus, such as his Sermon on the Mount. From the New Testament we will also look at the Letters of St. Paul, which are an important source of Christian ethical teaching. These ancient sources are the roots from which the Catholic ethical tradition will grow.

The ancient Roman Empire fell, but the Catholic Church lived on, and it continued to develop during the years 475 to 1400, which is considered the medieval period of history. During the medieval period, Catholic moral theologians and Catholic philosophers continued to refine and elaborate Catholic ethics. In the medieval period, these developments and insights were gathered in summaries of theology and ethics, such as the *Summa Theologiae* (1240) by Alexander of Hales and the *Summa Contra Gentiles* (1264) and the *Summa Theologiae* (1274), both written by Thomas Aquinas. We will look at these kinds of developments and insights in chapter 2 of *CFE*, on medieval Catholic ethics.

As the modern era dawned, the Catholic tradition persisted. During the modern period between 1400 and 1900, many manuals of moral theology were composed for the purpose of providing the necessary and basic elements of Catholic ethics for modern readers. These manuals, such as *Institutiones Morales* (1602), written by Juan Azor, were used to teach people (and priests) the basics of Catholic ethics. As compared with the summaries of the medieval period, though, these manuals were simplified and did not contain all of the dimensions of Catholic ethics. This era of modern Catholic ethics will be the focus of chapter 3 of *CFE*.

In the contemporary period of the twentieth and twenty-first centuries, the limitations of these modern manuals were identified. So, in 1992, the Catholic Church published a new and more comprehensive *Catholic Catechism*, in which it sought to present the entirety of Catholic teaching in terms of faith and morals. Additionally, in 2005 the Catholic Church published a *Compendium of Catholic Social Teaching*. The *Compendium* is a work that offers a comprehensive collection of Catholic ethical teachings. Chapter 4 of *CFE* will review the main ethical concepts and principles of these two important contemporary Catholic works on ethics.

Diagram I.I

Time Period	Ancient (1000 BCE to 475 CE)	Medieval (475 CE to 1400)	Modern (1400 to 1900)	Contemporary (1900 to present)
Important Ethical Sources	Old Testament New Testament	Summas	Manuals	Catechism of 1992 Compendium of 2005

The Franciscan Tradition

The Catholic ethical tradition thus has persisted since ancient times, through many centuries of refinement and development (see diagram I.I). In this overall framework, where does the Franciscan tradition begin? It begins with the life, teachings, and ethical and spiritual insights of St. Francis of Assisi (1181–1226), who lived in the medieval period of Catholic history.

Chapter 5 of CFE describes how St. Francis participates in the Catholic ethical tradition and works to renew and revitalize what it means to be an ethical Christian. Francis' ethical and spiritual vision was carried forward into the modern and contemporary periods of Catholic history by Franciscans, followers of Francis.

Chapter 6, the final chapter of CFE, applies Catholic Franciscan ethics to particular ethical issues—both personal ethical issues and social ethical issues. Some of these issues include respect and care for self, for human life, for the marginalized, and for the earth. Note that key concepts, review questions, and discussion questions are provided at the end of each chapter.

Ethical Concepts, Principles, Theories, and Traditions

In addition to a historical framework, CFE offers another framework with which to organize and understand the Catholic and Franciscan ethical traditions. This book is an introductory-level text, so it describes the basic ethical concepts, ethical principles, and ethical theories that are found in the Catholic and Franciscan ethical traditions.

Ethical concepts are the fundamental building blocks of ethics. In this book we will look at a variety of ethical concepts, including virtue, happiness, natural law, command, rights, duty, freedom, etc. *Ethical principles* we will look at include "the Golden Rule" and the principle "the end does not justify the means." *Ethical theories* tie together ethical concepts and principles. In this book we will look at the following ethical theories: virtue ethics theory, natural law ethical theory, deontological ethical theory, and the theory of the ethics of care.

I will end this short introduction with a prayer written by St. Francis of Assisi in 1205. It is simply called "The Prayer before the Crucifix." As you read it, note some of the ethical concepts that are mentioned.

Most High,
glorious God,
enlighten the darkness of my heart
and give me
true faith,
certain hope,
and perfect charity,
sense and knowledge,
Lord,
that I may carry out
Your holy and true command.

1

ANCIENT CATHOLIC ETHICS

There was a scholar of the law who stood up to test Jesus and said, "Teacher, what must I do to inherit eternal life?" Jesus said to him, "What is written in the law? How do you read it?" The scholar said in reply, "You shall love the Lord, your God, with all your heart, with all your being, with all your strength, and with all your mind, and your neighbor as yourself." Jesus replied to him, "You have answered correctly; do this and you will live."

But because the scholar wished to justify himself, he said to Jesus, "And who is my neighbor?" Jesus replied, "A man fell victim to robbers as he went down from Jerusalem to Jericho. They stripped and beat him and went off leaving him half dead. A priest happened to be going down that road, but when he saw him, he passed by on the opposite side. Likewise a Levite came to the place, and when he saw him, he passed by on the opposite side. But a Samaritan traveler who came upon him was moved with compassion at the sight. He approached the victim, poured oil and wine over his wounds and bandaged them. Then he lifted him up on his own animal, took him to an inn and cared for him. The next day he took out two silver coins and gave them to the innkeeper with the instruction, 'Take care of him. If you spend more than what I have given you, I shall repay you on my way back.'

"Which of these three, in your opinion, was neighbor to the robbers' victim?" Jesus asked. The scholar answered, "The one who treated him with mercy." Jesus said to him, "Go and do likewise."

This story that Jesus tells in order to answer the scholar's question is known as the Parable of the Good Samaritan. A parable is a comparison between two things, used to illustrate a moral or religious truth, frequently in the form of a story. This particular parable of Jesus appears in the Gospel of Luke, Chapter 10, verses 25–37. The Gospel of Luke is a book in the Bible that appears in the New Testament, alongside three other Gospels: Matthew, Mark, and John. All four of the Gospels describe the life of Jesus: what he did, what he said, and what he taught.

At the beginning of the Parable of the Good Samaritan, Jesus asks the scholar what he believed was written in "the law." This is an obvious reference to the law of the Old Testament. The first five books of the Old Testament (Genesis, Exodus, Leviticus, Numbers, and Deuteronomy) are known as the "books of the law"; they contain the laws given by God to Moses on Mount Sinai in Egypt (see diagram 1.1). In those early and ancient books of the Bible we find the Ten Commandments that God gave to Moses. The Ten Commandments appear in the book of Exodus (20:2–17) and the book of Deuteronomy (5:6–21) (see diagram 1.2). In the Parable of the Good Samaritan when the scholar says that the law says to "love the Lord your God with all your heart," the scholar is referring to the first commandment that appears in the Old Testament.

Diagram 1.1

Important Sources of Ancient Catholic Ethics	
The Old Testament of the Bible	The New Testament of the Bible
Contains 46 books, including Genesis, Exodus, Psalms, Job, Daniel, Isaiah, etc.	Contains 27 books, including the Gospels of Mark, Matthew, Luke and John; the Acts of the Apostles; the 13 letters of St. Paul; the Book of Revelation, etc.

In the next section, we will only focus on the ethical concepts and principles that appear in the oldest parts of the Bible, the Old Testament, which were written roughly one thousand years before the time of Jesus.

Diagram 1.2

The Ten Commandments

1. I am the Lord your God: you shall not have strange Gods before me.
2. You shall not take the name of the Lord your God in vain.
3. Remember to keep holy the Lord's Day.
4. Honor your father and your mother.
5. You shall not kill.
6. You shall not commit adultery.
7. You shall not steal.
8. You shall not bear false witness against your neighbor.
9. You shall not covet your neighbor's wife.
10. You shall not covet your neighbor's goods.

1.1 The Ten Commandments

The very first book of the Bible is Genesis; it was given that name because it describes the origins of the world. In the book of Genesis we find the basic foundational belief in the Catholic tradition that God is the creator who created the heavens and the earth and saw them as good.

Genesis makes clear that God is the creator of all reality, including human reality. Another important foundational belief in the Catholic tradition that is found in Genesis is the belief that human beings are made in the image and likeness of God.

> *Then God said: "Let us make man in our image, after our likeness"* …
> *God created man in his image; in the divine image he created him; male and female he created them.* (Genesis 1:26–27)

These two foundational beliefs—that God is creator and that human beings are made in the image and likeness of God—are not in themselves *ethical* beliefs or statements. They are beliefs about the world and about human nature, which serve as important foundations and backgrounds for Catholic ethics. To see how ethical beliefs and statements differ from statements about the world, consider this initial and basic definition of ethics.

> Ethics: *Guidelines about how we should live, guidelines about right and wrong.*

When people think of the word *ethics* they usually think "right and wrong." And that's accurate. Ethical right and wrong are about what *should* be done.

And ethical guidelines are about what people *should* do. Ethics—whether ethical beliefs, statements, or guidelines—is unique in this way. Ethics doesn't merely *describe* how people behave, but it is about how people *should* behave.

Whereas beliefs and statements about the world describe the world and the things in the world, including human beings (e.g., God created the world, God created humans, humans are made in God's image), *ethical* beliefs and statements are about what we should do.

The Old Testament states that God, by giving commandments to Moses, tells human beings what they should do. Moses then has the responsibility of sharing the commandments with all of humanity. So the first and best place to look for ethics in the Old Testament is in the Ten Commandments.

A *commandment* or *command* is an important aspect of ethics. It is particularly important for Christian ethics, because if God the creator issues a command to someone (that someone is clearly a being that God has created, since God created everything), then that person feels obligated to obey the command. Ethics are guidelines for how to live; so then obviously, when God commands his people to perform particular kinds of actions, then that is what his people *should* do.

Another important ethical concept that connects to the concept of command is *duty*. A duty is something one is required to do; it is a responsibility, an obligation. The very act of God commanding humans to act in a particular way establishes which duties humans have. The Ten Commandments, then, state our basic duties we have regarding God and other human beings.

It is very straightforward to look at the Ten Commandments as providing an ethical code for the ancient Israelites. With the Ten Commandments, God has revealed himself to his people and has indicated what he wants his people to do. To follow the commandments is to cooperate with God's plan.

Notice that the first three of the commandments are about how human beings should behave toward God; they state our duties to God. The other seven commandments are about how human beings should treat each other; they state our duties to others. Some of the Ten Commandments tell us what we should do (e.g., keep holy the Lord' day, honor your father and mother, etc.), whereas other commands tell us what we should *not* do (e.g., you shall not kill, you shall not bear false witness against your neighbor, etc.).

To get a sense of how the Ten Commandments provide guidance for how to live, let us look at each commandment and consider how the Catholic tradition links the commandment to specific actions. The first three commandments are about our duties to God. So what do these commandments point out as our duties, the things we should do? Here are some examples, and there are many, many more. A basic duty we have to God is to believe in him (first commandment); a second basic duty we have to God is to respect his name and hold it as sacred (second); a third basic duty we have to God is to make an outward sign of keeping his day holy by attending mass on Sundays (third).

The other seven commandments address how we ought to act toward other humans. We have a duty to respect our parents (fourth); respect each human person as an image of God (fifth); respect one's God-given sexual powers and strive to preserve one's marriage (sixth); respect other people's property and the goods of creation (seventh); tell the truth (eighth); have a pure heart and pure intention with regard to sexuality (ninth); and have a pure heart and pure intention with regard to other people's property (tenth).

In this quick overview we can see how the Ten Commandments offer a rich ethic, a fairly comprehensive guideline for how we should live. The Ten Commandments clearly lay out the outlines of a good ethical life. The Catholic tradition views this ethical outline as one of God's gifts to humanity. Over time, Catholic ethics becomes filled in with more and more layers of detail.

1.2 The Gospels

The Catholic tradition views Jesus as another great gift to humanity. The New Testament of the Bible, which was written roughly between the years 50 to 150, describes the life and teachings of Jesus. Jesus lived during the time of the ancient Roman Empire, and it was the ancient Roman authorities who eventually crucified him.

The word *gospel* is a translation of a Greek word that means "good news." The Gospels are four books of the Bible that describe the words and actions of Jesus; they include accounts of his birth, his preaching, his suffering, and his resurrection. The four Gospels of Mark, Matthew, Luke, and John convey the good news that Jesus has lived among us, and has showed us the truth about what it means to be human. In this section we will focus on a sermon that Jesus preached on the side of a mountain somewhere in Galilee, in northern

Israel. It is known as the Sermon on the Mount, and it sums up many of his teachings (Gospel of Matthew, chapters 5, 6, and 7).

Jesus addresses the sermon to a large crowd. Consistent with the Genesis statement that humans are made in the image and likeness of God, Jesus regarded each individual as important, even those who had a low social standing in his society, such as peasants, women, fishermen, tax collectors, lepers, and prostitutes.

Jesus begins his Sermon on the Mount with nine statements that have a poetic symmetry. Each of the statements begins with the word *blessed* (or *happy* in some translations of the Bible); so, from the Latin word *beatitudinem*, which means "state of blessedness," this series of statements is called the Beatitudes (see diagram 1.3). The Beatitudes sum up, according to the teachings of Jesus, what a blessed and happy life is like, and they are the heart of Jesus' preaching. As you can tell from the last line of the Beatitudes, they outline a path that leads to heaven. With the Beatitudes, Jesus offers an answer to the traditional philosophical questions that all human beings ask themselves: "What is happiness?" and "What is true happiness?" *Philosophy* literally means "love of wisdom" (*philo* = "love," *sophy* = "wisdom"), and it is an activity of investigation that seeks true answers to basic questions about human beings and all of reality.

Diagram 1.3

The Beatitudes

1. Blessed are the poor in spirit, for theirs is the kingdom of heaven.
2. Blessed are those who mourn, for they shall be comforted.
3. Blessed are the meek, for they shall inherit the earth.
4. Blessed are those who hunger and thirst for righteousness, for they shall be satisfied.
5. Blessed are the merciful, for they shall obtain mercy.
6. Blessed are the pure in heart, for they shall see God.
7. Blessed are the peacemakers, for they shall be called sons of God.
8. Blessed are those who are persecuted for righteousness sake, for theirs is the kingdom of heaven.
9. Blessed are you when men revile you and persecute you and utter all kinds of evil against you falsely on my account. Rejoice and be glad, for your reward is great in heaven.

Matthew 5:3–12

Happiness, as defined by Jesus in the Beatitudes, has a supernatural dimension to it; that is, an ethical life is not necessarily one that will lead you to happiness and blessedness in your earthly life. A happy and blessed life may only come to you in heaven. Along with command and duty, *happiness* is another important ethical concept in ancient Catholic ethics.

Using happiness as a touchstone, let's look at how the Beatitudes offer ethical guidance. Human beings have a natural desire for happiness. So we could think of Jesus as saying: "You desire happiness, right? Well, happiness includes being meek, merciful, pure in heart, and a peacemaker." So what should you do to achieve the happiness you naturally desire? Be someone who is meek (humble), and not arrogant. Be someone who is merciful, not unforgiving. Be someone who is pure in heart, not divided in one's heart, or deceitful. Be a peacemaker, not a hostile and aggressive person. With the Beatitudes, Jesus is suggesting particular character traits we could develop that will in the process lead us to happiness and blessedness. As we will see later in this chapter (section 1.4), traditionally these kinds of traits are known as *virtues*, another important ethical concept.

In the Sermon on the Mount Jesus refers to the law of the Old Testament and the Ten Commandments, as he did in the Parable of the Good Samaritan. In the Sermon, he refers to some of the Ten Commandments specifically:

> You have heard that it was said to your ancestors, "You shall not kill" ... But I say to you, whoever is angry with his brother will be liable to judgment. (Matthew 5:21–22)

> You have heard that it was said, "You shall not commit adultery" ... But I say to you, everyone who looks at a woman with lust has already committed adultery with her in his heart. (Matthew 5:27–28)

In these two examples, Jesus is obviously referring to commandments five and six. Commandment five, when phrased as "do not kill," seems to focus on the *human action* of killing. Commandment six, too, when phrased as "do not commit adultery," seems to focus on the *action* of adultery.

Think back to commandments nine and ten for a moment, about not "coveting" your neighbor's wife or goods, which are about having a pure heart and pure intention. With commandments nine and ten the focus is on intention and motive, not so much on a particular action. So, too, Jesus shows us in this Sermon that we can think of the other commandments in this way as well. He is saying that it is true that we should not kill, but in addition we should not allow ourselves to be overcome with particular emotions that might move us to kill, such as anger. And while it is true that we should not commit the act of adultery (which is sexual relations between a married person and someone other than his or her spouse, by the way), we should also not allow ourselves to be overcome with particular emotions that might move us to commit adultery, such as lust.

Ethics, then, involves what privately goes on inside us—our internal thoughts, our intentions, and our motives—and not only our outward and external public actions. In this way Jesus further deepens the ethic outlined in the Ten Commandments and emphasizes the importance of the human heart, the deepest root of human action. In another part of the Sermon on the Mount where he talks about almsgiving (donating to the needy), Jesus makes a similar contrast between our internal private lives and our external public actions. He says we don't need to advertise and brag that we are donating to the needy. It's fine if our almsgiving is done in secret, because, after all, God the Father sees our secrets. According to Jesus, God knows all our actions and all of our thoughts and prayers (Matthew 6:2–6).

In the Sermon, Jesus teaches that for ethics the most important internal emotional state is love. Here is the first time love is mentioned in the Sermon:

> You have heard that it was said, "You shall love your neighbor and hate your enemy." But I say to you, love your enemies, and pray for those who persecute you. (Matthew 5:43–44)

Usually when Jesus says "you have heard that it was said," he is referring to something in the Old Testament. In this case, he may be referring to a passage from the Old Testament's book of Psalms where it says:

> If only you would destroy the wicked, O God, and the men of blood were to depart from me! Wickedly they invoke your name; your foes swear faithless oaths. Do I not hate, O Lord, those who hate you? Those who rise up against you do I not loathe? With a deadly hatred I hate them; they are my enemies. (Psalms 139:19–22)

Although we might naturally feel that we hate our enemies, Jesus is commanding us to love our enemies. Jesus' command is about what we *should* do. So Jesus is making an *ethical* statement about loving our enemies. He is not saying that we *do* love our enemies, because as the speaker in Psalm 139 is saying, we might actually feel that we really do hate our enemies. The statement "I hate my enemies" might accurately describe me right now. Yet, Jesus' ethics, as guidelines about how we should live, and guidelines about right and wrong, tell us that we *should* love our enemies; it is ethically right for us to do so.

But it isn't only our enemies that we should love, of course. Jesus says we should love our neighbors, too—we should simply love one another (John 13:34). To love one another and to love our enemies, as a guideline for how to live one's life, is extremely challenging. But for Jesus, the fact that it is challenging doesn't mean that it is not the right thing to do. No one said living ethically had to be easy. Jesus has set the ethical standard very high, and he realizes it. After the part of the Sermon where he says to love our neighbors and our enemies he then says:

> So be perfect, just as your heavenly Father is perfect. (Matthew 5:48)

Jesus knows that we are imperfect, we are sinners, and that "to err is human." Yet his ethic tells us to strive toward perfection. We know we'll never actually "be perfect," but striving to be as perfect as we can is something we nevertheless *should* do.

When Jesus was asked which commandment is the greatest, he said:

> You shall love the Lord, your God, with all your heart, with all your soul, and with all your mind. This is the greatest and the first commandment. The second is like it: You shall love your neighbor as yourself. (Matthew 22:37–39; Mark 12:28–31)

This is very similar to what we have seen in the Parable of the Good Samaritan. There, Jesus also referred back to the commandments of the Old Testament and summed them up in terms of love. As we have seen with the Beatitudes, Jesus deepens the ethic outlined in the Ten Commandments by emphasizing the importance of the human heart, which is the deepest root of human action. And Jesus recommends that love should be our deepest motivator. In all that we do, we should do it out of love. Whereas the first commandment in the Old Testament says "I am the Lord your God: you shall not have strange Gods before me," Jesus sums it up as saying "You shall love the Lord, your God, with all your heart, with all your soul, and with all your mind." And whereas the seven commandments about how we should treat others do outline various duties we have (honor your parents, do not steal, do not kill, etc.), Jesus sums up those seven commandments as saying "You shall love your neighbor as yourself." We can regard Jesus' teachings that we find in the Gospels as an ethics of love. And it fits with viewing God not only as creator and commander, but as love itself.

John, who wrote one of the Gospels, also wrote some letters that appear in the New Testament of the Bible. In John's first letter, twice he writes:

"*God is love.*" (*1 John 4:8, 16*)

The Catholic tradition views Jesus' teaching on love as a twofold commandment. It is a commandment of love with two parts: the first part is the command to love God, and the second part is a command to love others (see diagram 1.4). *Charity* is a traditional term for this kind of love that Jesus is talking about, so Jesus' twofold commandment of love can be called the *ethical principle of charity*.

Diagram 1.4

Jesus' Twofold Commandment of Love (Principle of Charity)	
Love God with all your heart.	1. I am the Lord your God. 2. You shall not take the name of the Lord in vain. 3. Remember to keep holy the Lord's Day.
Love your neighbor as yourself.	4. Honor your father and your mother. 5. You shall not kill. 6. You shall not commit adultery. 7. You shall not steal. 8. You shall not bear false witness. 9. You shall not covet your neighbor's wife. 10. You shall not covet your neighbor's goods.

In his Sermon on the Mount, Jesus also states another important ethical principle, the principle of the Golden Rule:

Do to others whatever you would have them do to you. (*Matthew 7:12; Luke 6:31*)

A slightly different version of the principle appears in the Old Testament book Tobit, as "Do to no one what you yourself dislike" (Tobit 15). Jesus states the ethical principle in a positive form, as about what we *should* do, whereas in Tobit the principle is put in a negative form, as about what we should *not* do ("Don't do to people what *you* dislike").

As we leave our discussion of the Gospels, we can summarize the ethical approach found there as centering on the ethical concepts of *command, happiness, virtues*, and *love (charity)* and two ethical principles, the *principle of charity* and the *principle of the Golden Rule*.

In the Gospel of Matthew it is described how, after Jesus has been crucified and then resurrected, he tells his closest followers:

> Go, therefore, and make disciples of all nations, baptizing them in the name of the Father, and of the Son, and of the holy Spirit, teaching them to observe all that I have commanded you. And behold, I am with you always, until the end of the age. (Matthew 28:19–20)

1.3 The Letters of Paul

St. Paul took Jesus at his word and made it his mission to spread Jesus' teaching as far and wide as he could. Paul was instrumental in helping to establish early Christian communities all over the Mediterranean region. The Gospels are the "good news," and Paul made it his mission to spread the good news as far as he could. Many of the letters that Paul sent to the various young Christian communities made their way into the New Testament. Of the twenty-seven books that make up the New Testament, thirteen of these books are letters attributed to St. Paul.

An important part of what Paul conveys in these letters concerns ethics. Think of the basic definition of ethics we have been using: ethics are guidelines about how we should live, guidelines about right and wrong. In his letters, Paul will often say things that clearly indicate that he means to be offering an ethic. In his letter to the Ephesians he says to "Watch carefully how you live" (Ephesians 5:15). In his first letter to the Thessalonians he says that he is describing "How you should conduct yourselves to praise God" (1 Thessalonians 4:1). Paul views the ethic he is describing as a new ethic that has been outlined by Jesus. He writes:

> Put away the old self of your former way of life, be renewed, you learned Christ and were taught in him. (Ephesians 4:20–24)

Paul is encouraging people to live differently, given what they have learned from Jesus. Since Paul seeks to spread the good news about Jesus and share what he knows about Jesus' teachings, it is appropriate that we should find much of Jesus' ethics that we discussed in the context of the Gospels reappearing in Paul's letters. Here are some examples:

> love one another ... Rejoice in hope, endure in affliction ... Bless those who persecute you, bless and do not curse them ... weep with those who weep ... do not be haughty but associate with the lowly. ... Do not repay anyone evil for evil ... live at peace with all ... if your enemy is hungry, feed him ... conquer evil with good. (Letter to the Romans 12:10–21)

> Put on then, as God's chosen ones, holy and beloved, heartfelt compassion, kindness, humility, gentleness, and patience ... forgiving one another. ... And over all these put on love, that is, the bond of perfection. And let the peace of Christ control your hearts. (Letter to the Colossians 3:12–15)

> I ... urge you to live in a manner worthy of the call you have received, with all humility and gentleness, with patience, bearing with another through love ... living the truth in love ... be kind to one another, compassionate, forgiving one another as God has forgiven you. (Letter to the Ephesians 4:1–32)

> You yourselves have been taught by God to love one another. (First Letter to the Thessalonians 4:9)

In these examples we can see how Paul echoes Jesus' Beatitudes and Jesus' teachings about an ethic of love. Paul encourages the early Christians to adopt Jesus' ethic of love, and like Jesus recommended, to view ethics as involving good actions as well as ethically pure intentions and motivations:

> Whatever you do, do from the heart. (Letter to the Colossians 3:23)

Paul calls Jesus "the image of the invisible God" (Colossians 1:15). Jesus said we should strive to be perfect like God is perfect and try to imitate God. Now Paul is pointing out that Jesus himself is the image of the invisible God. It follows, then, that if we try to imitate Jesus, we will be striving to imitate God. In Paul's letters, the person of Jesus is portrayed as our model for what a good person is. As Paul puts it:

> So be imitators of God ... and live in love, as Christ loved us and handed himself over for us as a sacrificial offering to God. (Ephesians 5:1–2).

With Paul's instruction for people to behave as Jesus behaved, Catholic ethics becomes even more richly detailed. We saw the Ten Commandments as the foundation, and then Jesus building on them and advocating an ethics of love; now Paul can say that Christian ethics simply consists in being like Jesus: striving to have the traits, qualities, and characteristics that Jesus has, imitating his actions, and following Jesus' guidance. This is what it means to live a Christian ethical life.

As we noted in section 1.3, the particular character traits that lead us to happiness and blessedness are traditionally called *virtues*. In the above excerpts from Paul's letters, the following virtues appear: love (charity), hope, humility, forgiveness (mercy), peacefulness, compassion, kindness, gentleness, and patience. Paul calls our attention to a particular set of virtues. By looking in detail at Christian virtues, Paul is helping us to get very specific about what it means to imitate Jesus. The Catholic tradition has identified the seven virtues of prudence, justice, fortitude, temperance, faith, hope, and love (charity) as the most important virtues, because all the other virtues are grouped around these seven. The first four were noted in the Old Testament (Wisdom 8:7), but it is only in the New Testament, when explicitly noted by Paul, that the last three come to be fully recognized. As Paul puts it:

> So faith, hope, love remain ... but the greatest of these is love. (1 Corinthians 13:13)

It should seem appropriate that Paul says the greatest and most important Christian virtue is love (charity), since love has such a prominent position in Jesus' ethics. In section 1.4 we will look at these seven Christian virtues in closer detail. But for now let us turn to a few more important aspects of Catholic ethics with roots in Paul's letters.

In this chapter we have noted that in ethics there are different ethical concepts that are closely related. A *virtue*, as a character trait, is different from a *human action*. And a *human action* is different from an *intention*. And all of these are different from *happiness/blessedness*. In his letter to the Romans (3:8), Paul states an ethical principle about *human actions*, and it has come to be known as the *Pauline principle*:

> One may not do evil so that good may result from it. (A good end does not justify an evil means).

This is a very general ethical principle that has many applications. To see how it works, consider the following example. Both Jesus and Paul advocate that we should live in peace. Let's say I agree with them, and I think that peace is an important good. Now, though, there is a troublemaker who keeps disturbing the peace. Maybe I should assassinate this troublemaker, so that I could achieve the good outcome of peace. The Pauline principle says that I should not do this evil action of assassinating someone, hoping to bring about the good of peace. Or, worded differently, bringing about the good of peace does not justify the evil action of assassinating someone.

In addition to writing about Jesus as the visible sign of the invisible God, Paul also writes of God revealed in other ways besides through Jesus. Notice in the following passage from Paul's letter to the Romans what Paul says about God and creation:

> There are those who suppress the truth with wickedness. But what can be known about God is evident to them, because God made it evident to them. Ever since the creation of the world, his invisible attributes of eternal power and divinity have been able to be understood and perceived in what he has made. As a result, they have no excuse, for although they knew God, they did not accord him glory as God, or give him thanks. (Romans 1:18–21)

The Catholic tradition views what Paul says here as an acknowledgment that human beings—even when not exposed to the Bible—can know about God by viewing and studying creation. Thus, simply by using human reason, the human mind has the potential to know of God.

Also, in another chapter of Paul's letter to the Romans, Paul notices that there are some people who do not have the Bible or the Old Testament law, and yet they seem to be following and observing the basic outlines of that law. How could this be? For Paul, their behavior shows that "the demands of the law are written in their hearts" (Romans 2:14–15). This view of Paul's would seem to be consistent with the Genesis passage about human beings as made in the image and likeness of God. God, as creator, molded human nature so that his law could be understood without having to be explicitly exposed to the law through the use of the Bible. Like the ability to know God by viewing and studying creation, humans are seen to have the ability to know God's law simply by using human reason. The Catholic tradition sums up Paul's teaching on this issue by saying that there are two basic ways of knowing about God and God's law: one, knowing by the use of reason and thinking, and two, knowing through faith in God and the Bible, which is the revealed word of God (see Diagram 1.5).

Diagram 1.5

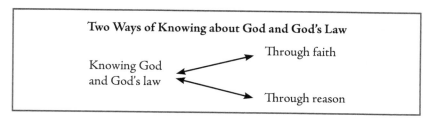

In the box:

Two Ways of Knowing about God and God's Law

Knowing God and God's law

Through faith

Through reason

1.4 Christian Virtues

In this chapter we have seen virtues come up a few different times, such as in the Beatitudes and in Paul's letters. The Parable of the Good Samaritan that opened the chapter even highlights some virtues. In the parable, the Samaritan is a person who exhibits the virtues of compassion, caring, and mercy.

In this section we will look in more detail at the most important Christian virtues and try to make better sense of them with an ethical theory known as *virtue ethics*. Virtue ethics can help tie together various ethical concepts, such as action, virtue, intention, and happiness.

As we have seen, a virtue is simply a trait or a characteristic of a person that leads to happiness, blessedness, or well-being. These characteristics and traits of a person can be called *virtues*. Another ancient term for these character traits is *perfections*. In the Sermon on the Mount Jesus said: "Be perfect, as your heavenly Father is perfect" (Matthew 5:48). God the Father is considered to have many perfections, such as all-loving, all-good, merciful, just, compassionate, humble, and patient. Jesus tells us to strive toward having the perfections that God has. And Jesus suggests specific perfections that lead to happiness/blessedness. Paul, then, tells us to strive toward having the perfections that Jesus has, since Jesus is the image of the invisible God. Virtue ethics views *role models* as very important, since with their example we can see for ourselves what particular virtues look like in real life. For Christian virtue ethics, Jesus is our most important role model.

By focusing on particular virtues, we can get more specific about how to imitate Jesus. The Catholic tradition has identified the following seven virtues as the most important virtues:

- Prudence
- Justice

- Fortitude
- Temperance
- Faith
- Hope
- Love (charity)

The first four are called cardinal virtues and are known as *moral virtues*. The virtue of *prudence* is the character trait of making good judgments in decision making. The virtue of *justice* is the character trait of giving others what they deserve, including respect for God and for other persons. The virtue of *fortitude* is the character trait of being determined and courageous, especially in the face of fear. The virtue of *temperance* is the character trait of balancing the attraction of pleasures, desires, and instincts.

These four virtues are acquired by human effort. One develops them by repeated actions. As we all know, repeated actions can become habits. Think of moral virtues as good habits that we can develop. We also know that some of our habits can be bad. Just as we can develop good habits, we can also develop bad habits. In ethics, moral virtues are considered good habits and *vices* are bad habits. Moral virtues are good habits because they lead to happiness and well-being, and vices are bad habits because they lead to unhappiness and misery.

The virtues of faith, hope, and charity (love) are not considered moral virtues, but are called *theological virtues* (*theo* means "God"). Theological virtues are not the result of habitual actions, but are instilled into human souls by God. Jesus, by placing emphasis on our internal moral life—our thoughts, intentions, and motives—paves the way for seeing how ethics has to do with our internal souls and the movement of the Holy Spirit within us. *Faith* is the virtue of believing in God and what he has revealed. *Hope* is the virtue of desiring eternal life in heaven. *Charity (love)* is the virtue of loving God and neighbor. Charity is a unique virtue; it can be present in all the rest of the virtues. Jesus' ethic of love is a virtue ethic, one that makes a particular virtue—charity—most important.

Now for a little more virtue theory to help tie things together. Virtue ethics is an ethical theory that wants us to focus on virtues, character traits of persons. We can contrast virtue ethics with action-centered ethical theories, which focus on human actions. For action theories, the main questions are: "What is the action?" "Was it right?" "Was it wrong?" To decide if the action is right or wrong, some action theories say to look at the person's intention in performing the action. Other action theories say to look at the outcome or end in order to determine if the action is right or wrong. Another way that action theories say to determine if an action is right or wrong is by using ethical principles. We can ask whether our action is consistent with the Ten Commandments, or the principle of the Golden Rule, or the Pauline principle, for instance.

Virtue-centered ethical analysis is more complicated; it basically incorporates action theory into the context of the whole person. Actions, intentions, outcomes, and principles are important, but so are repeated actions, virtues, and one's overall character. Intentions and actions, when repeated, can become good habits, or virtues. Virtues (or vices) become part of one's *character*, what kind of person one is. What kind of person one is, in turn, leads to outcomes, such as happiness, unhappiness, blessedness, well-being, or misery (see diagram 1.6).

Diagram 1.6

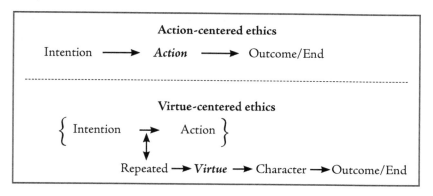

1.5 Conclusion

In this chapter we have covered a lot of ground. Several foundational beliefs about God and human nature stand out. God is the creator and God is love. Human beings, a unique part of God's creation, are made in the image and likeness of God. Human beings can make decisions and decide how they will act and what kind of persons they wish to be. The basic definition of ethics we are using is that ethics are guidelines about how we should live, guidelines about right and wrong. At the root of any ethical guideline are the most basic ethical questions: How should we live? What should we do?

These are philosophical questions. And the ancient Catholic tradition offers well-developed answers to these philosophical questions.

According to ancient Catholic ethics, to see how we should live and what we should do we need to consider the Ten Commandments of the Old Testament and be familiar with the basic duties they set out for us. We should also consider the New Testament: the teachings of Jesus that are found in the Gospels, including the Beatitudes and the Sermon on the Mount, as well as Paul's restatements of Jesus' teaching that appear in his many letters. Through the New Testament we can see that for ancient Catholic ethics how we should live has to do with actions and duties as well as with our inner spiritual life: our feelings, our thoughts, our emotions, and our relationship with God. To know how to live, ancient Catholic ethics suggests becoming familiar with the person of Jesus. Jesus is described as our most important role model, who exemplifies many virtues that we ourselves can seek to develop.

The ancient period spanned many centuries. In the next chapter we will move out of the ancient world into the medieval period, which was another very long period of history, spanning roughly from the years 475 to 1400. During the medieval period Catholic theologians and philosophers start with the insights of ancient Catholic ethics and develop and elaborate ethical principles and theories that become essential parts of Catholic ethics as we know it today.

Concepts, Principles, Theories, and Traditions Introduced in Chapter 1

Concepts

Parable of the Good Samaritan

Ethics

Should

Human action

Motive/intention

Virtue

Vice

Moral virtue

Theological virtue

Right/wrong

Command

Duty

Happiness, the good life

Philosophy

Love (charity)

Habit

Role model

Character

Principles

Principle of the Golden Rule

Principle of charity

Pauline principle

Theories

Action-centered ethics

Virtue-centered ethics

Traditions

Catholic Christian ethics tradition

Review Questions

1. What was Jesus trying to show with the Parable of the Good Samaritan?
2. What two beliefs about the world are foundational to Catholic ethics? Explain how they are not ethical beliefs.
3. Explain how the concepts of *command* and *duty* work together.
4. According to Jesus' teachings, what do the Beatitudes have to do with human happiness?

5. How does Jesus' twofold commandment of love tie in with the Ten Commandments?

6. What are the seven most important Christian virtues? How do *moral virtues* differ from *theological virtues*?

7. How does the saying "practice makes perfect" fit well with virtue ethics?

Discussion Questions

1. Some of the Ten Commandments tell us what we should do (e.g., keep holy the Lord's Day, honor your father and mother, etc.), whereas other commands tell us what we should *not* do (e.g., you shall not kill, you shall not bear false witness against your neighbor, etc.). Section 1.1 describes duties that flow from the Ten Commandments and expresses all ten examples as things we *should* do. Describe the duties that flow from the Ten Commandments in different language, highlighting what we should *not* do.

2. Section 1.2 describes a few virtues that are highlighted in the Beatitudes. What are they? And what vices do they contrast with? Which other virtues or vices can you detect in the Beatitudes?

3. Section 1.2 says that commandments five and six can be phrased as focused on particular *actions*, and Jesus shows how to deepen our understanding of them by shifting our focus to the internal emotions and intentions that motivate these actions. Describe how two other commandments can be phrased so as to focus on action, and then can be rephrased so as to focus on emotion/intention/motive.

4. The chapter mentions that the ethical questions "What is true happiness?" and "How should I live?" are philosophical questions. Another example of an ethical philosophical question is "Where do ethical standards and guidelines ultimately come from?" Explain how the Catholic tradition answers this philosophical question; then, describe a different possible answer to this question.

5. Some philosophical questions focus on human nature; for example, "What is human nature?" "What are human beings?" and "What is a human person?" How does the ancient Catholic ethical tradition answer these philosophical questions?

6. Section 1.3 applies the Pauline principle to peace. Describe a different application of the Pauline principle.

2

MEDIEVAL CATHOLIC ETHICS

C atholic ethics was set on its foundation in the ancient world, in the Bible. Consider the following parable of Jesus that he offered at the very end of his Sermon on the Mount. Think about this parable in terms of what it implies about the Catholic ethical tradition.

> Everyone who listens to these words of mine and acts on them will be like a wise man who built his house on rock. The rain fell, the floods came, and the winds blew and buffeted the house. But it did not collapse; it had been set solidly on rock. And everyone who listens to these words of mine but does not act on them will be like a fool who built his house on sand. The rain fell, the floods came, and the winds blew and buffeted the house. And it collapsed and was completely ruined. (Matthew 7:24–27)

The very subject of ethics is discussed in this parable. Jesus is suggesting how we should act: we should act according to the teachings he offered. If we follow Jesus' teachings and put his ethics into action, then, according to the parable, we will have built our life (our house) on solid rock. Similarly, if the Catholic tradition itself puts Jesus' ethics into action, then it, too, will have been built on solid rock. Medieval philosophers and theologians agreed that a wise man would build his life on the teachings of Jesus, and they tried to explain how to do that. In this chapter we will focus on how two of these thinkers, St. Augustine (354–430), from the early medieval period, and St. Thomas Aquinas (1225–1274), who came later, both restated and further developed the ethical teachings of Jesus.

2.1 Catholic Moral Theology

Theology is a systematic reflection on one's faith (*theo* means "God"). *Moral theology* is a systematic reflection on the way of life taught by one's religion. St. Augustine of Hippo, North Africa, was a very influential theologian, moral theologian, and philosopher. Augustine lived at a time when Christianity was still in the process of being recognized as a major religion. In the year 325 the Catholic Church held a large council at Nicaea in western Turkey to define official Christian beliefs. At that council the Nicene Creed was created. The Nicene Creed states the most important parts of the Catholic faith, and reciting the Nicene Creed became a part of Christian worship (see diagram 2.1). Notice how the Nicene Creed is purely theological (as opposed to ethical); it is a series of statements about God—the Father, the Son, and the Holy Spirit. Part of Augustine's writings concern clarifying the differences between various Christian groups and how Christianity is unique among various religions.

Diagram 2.1

The Nicene Creed (325/381)

(also known as Profession of Faith)

I believe in one God, the Father almighty,
maker of heaven and earth, of all things visible and invisible.

And in one Lord Jesus Christ, the Only Begotten Son of God,
born of the Father before all ages.

God from God, Light from Light, true God from true God,
begotten, not made, consubstantial with the Father;
through him all things were made.

For us men and for our salvation he came down from heaven,
and by the Holy Spirit was incarnate of the Virgin Mary,
and became man.

For our sake he was crucified under Pontius Pilate,
he suffered death and was buried,
and rose again on the third day in accordance with the Scriptures.

He ascended into heaven and is seated at the right hand of the Father.
He will come again in glory to judge the living and the dead
and his kingdom will have no end.

I believe in the Holy Spirit, the Lord, the giver of life,
who proceeds from the Father and the Son,
who with the Father and the Son is adored and glorified,
who has spoken through the prophets.

I believe in one, holy, catholic and apostolic Church.

I confess one baptism for the forgiveness of sins
and I look forward to the resurrection of the dead
and the life of the world to come.

Revised translation, 2011.

Augustine was very familiar with ancient Greek and Roman philosophy, and he did not hesitate to use concepts and tools developed by those earlier philosophers to help clarify and defend his Christian worldview. Catholic moral theologians such as Augustine and Aquinas thought that using resources from non-Christian philosophers was quite appropriate. Paul, in his Letter to the Philippians, said:

> *Finally, brothers, whatever is true, whatever is honorable, whatever is just, whatever is pure, whatever is lovely, whatever is gracious, if there is any excellence and if there is anything worthy of praise, think about these things. (Philippians 4:8)*

Also, in Paul's first letter to the Thessalonians, he said:

> *Test everything; retain what is good. (1 Thessalonians 5:21)*

So if there was anything of excellence in the writings of the non-Christian philosophers, then, according to Paul's urging, we should consider it, test it, and use what is valuable.

As a Catholic moral theologian, Augustine's primary focus, though, was on understanding ethics as it was laid out in the Bible. In the year 397

Augustine wrote an autobiography entitled *The Confessions* in which he traces the events in his life, including how he converted to Christianity. As he writes the work, he speaks as if he is confessing his sins to God.

One of the sins that Augustine confesses in this work is something he did in his youth. He and some teenage friends stole pears from a neighbor's tree. Notice in this passage when discussing theft Augustine refers to ethical concepts from the Old and New Testament.

> Beyond question, theft is punished by your law, O Lord, and by the law written in human hearts, which not even sin itself can erase; for does any thief tolerate being robbed by another thief, even if he is rich and the other is driven by want? (Augustine 397, bk 2, chp 4)

When Augustine says that theft is "punished by your law, O Lord," he is referring to the seventh commandment from the Old Testament. When he says that it is also written in human hearts, he is referring to a concept from Paul's letter in the New Testament. As it appeared in Paul's letter, and again here in Augustine, the idea that ethics is rooted in the commandments *and* in human nature will continue throughout the Catholic ethical tradition.

Augustine wrote about ethics in many of his works. He wrote a commentary on the Sermon on the Mount, for instance, and he claimed that in the Sermon lies a complete and perfect teaching on Christian morality, a perfect model for Christian living. In the Sermon on the Mount Jesus states the Beatitudes about happiness. Augustine affirms that humans have a natural desire for happiness:

> We all certainly desire to live happily; and there is no human being but assents to this statement almost before it is made. (388, chp 3, verse 4)

Augustine wants to make clear that true human happiness comes through relationship with God. Humans naturally desire happiness because they naturally desire what is good. The highest and best happiness will come through loving the highest good.

But what is "the good"? Here is Augustine's answer:

> the good plainly exists; and we have shown by reasoning, as far as we were able, and by the divine authority which goes beyond our reasoning, that it is nothing else but God Himself ... to whom we can cleave only by affection, desire, and love. (388, chp 14, verse 24)

So what should we do to achieve that happiness that we naturally desire? Augustine says:

> *Following after God is the desire of happiness; to reach God is happiness itself. We follow after God by loving Him. (388, chp 11, verse 18)*

Augustine affirms the *principle of charity*—Jesus' twofold commandment of love: to achieve happiness we ought to love God and our neighbour as ourselves.

In keeping with the Genesis statement that humans are made in the image and likeness of God, since God has freedom and free will, so do human beings. Augustine writes that we should consider our ability to make free choices one of the good gifts from God.

> *free will is to be numbered among good things, and indeed not among the least of them, and therefore that it was given to us by God, who acted rightly in giving it. (387, bk 3, verse 1)*

We can achieve happiness with our free will by embracing God's law. It is right to do so and it is the path to true happiness. But because we have freedom, it is possible for us to act wrongly and unethically, to *sin*, which, at its root, is to simply turn away from God. We can turn away from God by disobeying his commands and by misdirecting our love away from God.

Although it is possible to achieve happiness with our free will, we cannot achieve our eternal reward without God's help. Augustine affirms St. Paul's claim that God's *grace* has an indispensable role in our ultimate happiness. In his Letter to the Ephesians, Paul wrote that

> *by grace you have been saved through faith, and this is not from you; it is the gift of God; it is not from works, so no one may boast. (Ephesians 2:8–9)*

As Augustine puts it:

> *Men are not saved by good works, nor by the free determination of their own will, but by the grace of God through faith. (421, chp 30)*

Augustine also made important contributions to Catholic virtue ethics and Jesus' ethics of love. In discussing the seven virtues, Augustine noted that the four moral virtues will be less than perfected if they are not connected with the three theological virtues. This is consistent with the idea that love/charity is the most important Christian virtue. For if one has prudence, for instance, but does not have love/charity, then one has not achieved one's highest potential. The way Augustine summed it up is that the four moral virtues of justice, temperance, fortitude, and prudence are actually four forms of love/charity (388, chp 15, verse 25). In this way, we can see that love/charity can be present in all of the virtues.

God is love and God is the highest good. The highest virtue, then, is perfect love of God. In taking the most important Christian virtue as the very definition of virtue itself, Augustine can say that he sees

> *virtue to be nothing else than perfect love of God. (388, chp 15, verse 25)*

God is the truth; so in loving God, according to Augustine, we love truth.

Another area of moral theology to which Augustine contributed is in regard to killing in wartime. It is true that "anyone who kills a human being, whether himself or anyone else, is involved in a charge of murder" (Augustine 413, bk 1, chp 21). Yet, Augustine argues that there are some exceptions to this. For instance,

> *one who owes a duty of obedience to the giver of the command does not himself "kill"—he is an instrument, a sword in its user's hand. For this reason the commandment forbidding killing was not broken by those who have waged wars on the authority of God. (413, bk 1, chp 21)*

Although the fifth commandment says you shall not kill, Augustine made the case that it is permissible to kill during war, as long as certain conditions are met. After Augustine, the Catholic tradition will continue to formulate these conditions, and the rationale for killing in wartime came to be called the *just war theory*.

2.2 Natural Law Ethics

After Augustine, the Catholic tradition of moral theology continued on for many centuries. St. Thomas Aquinas (1225–1274) picks up all of the ethical components we have looked at so far, including Augustine's contributions, and then pushes Catholic ethics further and further with more detail and argument.

Just as part of Augustine's writings concern clarifying basic dimensions of the Christian religion, the same is true with Aquinas, nearly nine hundred years later. In 1264, for instance, Aquinas composed a book called *On the Truth of the Catholic Faith*, its subtitle is *Summa Contra Gentiles*, and in the introduction he says:

> *I have set myself the task of making known, as far as my limited powers will allow, the truth that the Catholic faith professes, and of setting aside the errors that are opposed to it. (1264, bk 1, chp 2, verse 2)*

In the medieval period a *summa* is a kind of book; it is a "summary" of a particular subject matter. During this period, many theologians composed this kind of book. Aquinas composed two of them. His second one, the *Summa Theologiae* (1274), "Summary of Theology," was meant as a summary of Christian belief. In its introduction, Aquinas says he intends to explain the Christian religion briefly and for beginners. Yet the work is so huge that today we find it broken up into five volumes, exceeding three thousand pages!

Aquinas' work has an important place in the Catholic ethical tradition. In addition to being large, Aquinas' works are very intricate, orderly, and highly structured. He aims to give a systematic treatment of all theological topics, including moral theology. The *Summa* is a work of many parts, and its format resembles an encyclopedia, since it has entries on a huge assortment of topics. All of the topics he discusses fall under the large umbrella terms of *theology* and *philosophy*. In the work, Aquinas poses philosophical and theological questions, describes how different authorities have offered answers to them, and then offers his own answers, while also responding to other answers that differ from his own.

The first part of his *Summa Theologiae*, I, focuses on God, creation, angels, and human beings. Its second part is divided into two. The first half, which is the first part of the second part, I-II, is about happiness, free will, human actions, emotions, virtues, sin, law, and grace. The second half, which is the second part of the second part, II-II, is about the theological virtues, peace, war, and more virtues. The third part of the *Summa*, III, is about Jesus' birth, death, and resurrection and Church sacraments.

As we have seen in chapters 1 and 2 of *CFE*, there are many components to Catholic ethics. Since Aquinas' *Summa* is a summary, we should expect to find all elements of Catholic ethics discussed there, and indeed we do. Let's take these ethical components chronologically as we have encountered them. We first looked at the Old Testament of the Bible. Aquinas calls what appears in the Old Testament the *old law*. What appears in the New Testament of the Bible he calls the *new law*. Since the entire Bible is the revealed word of God, we can refer to *all* that appears in the Bible as *divine law*; it is the law that God reveals to human beings through scriptures. Besides divine law, Aquinas recognizes that there are different kinds of law, and several of them are important for ethics (see diagram 2.2).

Diagram 2.2

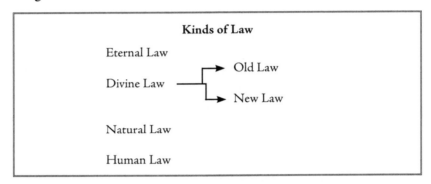

Another kind of law that Aquinas identifies, one that is even older and more ancient than the Old Law, is the *eternal law*. Aquinas finds this kind of law described by Augustine (387, bk 1, verse 6). The eternal law is an example of a kind of law that can come to be known by human beings simply through the use of their reason. The eternal law is so old because it is the very law that God used to organize the universe from the very origins of creation. As we have seen, the Catholic tradition views God as creator, God as commander, God as love, and now Aquinas is pointing out that God is divine reason. God created the world with a plan in mind, and just as St. Paul pointed out, we can see traces of God's plan simply by looking at the world around us and thinking about it. The world around us is obviously ordered and governed by "God the Ruler of the universe," says Aquinas (1274, I-II Q91, article 1). God's reason has always existed, which means that God's plan for the world has always existed. This plan, as God understands it, is the *eternal law*. Aquinas explains:

> *Although the eternal law is unknown to us according as it is in the Divine Mind: nevertheless, it becomes known to us somewhat ... by natural reason. (1274, I-II, Q19, article 4)*

Another kind of law that can come to be known through natural reason is the *natural law*. As we have said, everything in the universe is subject to God's plan, the eternal law. Rational creatures, though, can come to understand and participate in the eternal law more so than any other creatures. For Aquinas, it is the natural law that guides human reason to see the difference between good and evil (1274, Q91, I-II, article 2). This is a development of Paul's observation that the moral law is "written on the human heart" and that human beings do not have to be exposed to the Bible to learn the difference between right and wrong. Even though we can use our free will to commit wrongdoing and to develop bad habits, Aquinas says that the natural law can never be removed or separated "from men's hearts" (1274, I-II, Q94, article 6).

The last kind of law that Aquinas identifies (that he also sees mentioned in Augustine's work) is what he calls *human law*. Human laws are particular laws devised by human reason. Think of governments, legislatures, and statutes and the particular laws that societies develop over time, either out of custom or to deal with a practical issues that arise between people. These humanly created laws are *human laws*. Ethically, we would hope that our society's human laws reflect and are consistent with natural law and divine law, but we know that sometimes the laws of one's society can conflict with natural and divine law. The Catholic tradition holds that we cannot trust human laws on their own, but that we must check human laws against natural and divine law. For Aquinas, a general concept that we can use to evaluate any kind of law is the concept of "the common good." Every law, he says, should be intended for "the common good" (1274, I-II, Q90, article 2).

Human laws obviously give us guidance about what we should do. Laws about speed limits tell us how fast we should drive, for example. As we saw in the previous chapter, divine law gives us guidance about what we should do, too, both the old law (from the Old Testament) and the new law (from the New Testament). But how about natural law? How does natural law give us guidance about what we should do? Aquinas is famous for developing a natural law understanding of ethics. Let us briefly consider how he does this.

As we have seen, the Catholic tradition views the natural law as "written on the human heart." Humans have a natural attraction to things that are good. Recall a very basic thing that everyone perceives as good—mentioned by Jesus in the Beatitudes up through Augustine—namely, *happiness*. We have a natural attraction to happiness, and Augustine and Aquinas underscore how the most fulfilling ultimate happiness is "eternal happiness" (Aquinas 1274, I-II, Q108, article 4).

In chapter 1 in discussing the Beatitudes we saw how talking about happiness naturally leads to a discussion of the *virtues*. The question is, what kind of person do I have to be, what kinds of traits (virtues) do I need, to be truly happy? Jesus recommends that we be humble, merciful, pure in heart, and peacemakers. In section 1.4, in closely looking at how virtues are developed, we saw that moral virtues are *habits*, the product of repeated *actions*. Aquinas recognizes all these dimensions of ethics and the close relationships between happiness, virtues, and actions.

Aquinas says that since happiness is to be gained through kinds of actions, we must examine human actions in detail in order to find out which actions lead to happiness and which do not (1274, I-II, Q6, intro). He writes:

> Since therefore happiness is to be gained by means of certain acts, we must in due sequence consider human acts, in order to know by what acts we may obtain happiness, and by what acts we are prevented from obtaining it ... all practical knowledge is incomplete unless it takes account of things in detail. (1274, I-II, Q6, intro)

Now here is where the concept of natural law comes in. The *natural law* guides human reason to see the difference between good and evil. As Aquinas views it, all human beings as part of their human nature have the natural ability to see the difference between good and evil. Human beings, just because of the very kind of creature they are, have particular *inclinations*. Our minds and bodies tend to behave in ways that have a directedness. The most basic directedness is, as we have seen, toward happiness. Now, Aquinas uses the theory of natural law to get more specific about these inclinations, these directions. Basically, God has created human beings so that they have a natural inclination toward good and away from evil. Here is how Aquinas puts it:

> all those things to which man has a natural inclination, are naturally apprehended by reason as being good ... and their contraries as evil, ... objects of avoidance. (1274, I-II, Q94, article 2)

To get more specific, then, which kinds of things do human beings have natural inclinations toward? Here are the basic natural inclinations that Aquinas observes in human nature:

in man there is first of all an inclination to good ... and by reason of this inclination ... is a means of preserving human life, and of warding off its obstacles.

... there is in man an inclination to ... sexual intercourse, education of offspring and so forth.

... there is in man ... a natural inclination to know the truth about God, and to live in society: and in this respect, whatever pertains to this inclination belongs to the natural law. (1274, I-II, Q94, article 2)

So, overall, the natural law can guide us about what we should do. If we pay attention to human natural inclinations and reflect on the goods they point to, then Aquinas thinks we can identify basic goods and values (that God has intended for us, whether we acknowledge that or not). In the above quotes we can see *four* basic categories of goods: life, sexual reproduction, sociability, and knowledge. Actions that promote and protect these goods are good actions, and actions that go against or destroy these goods are bad actions.

Once we have this natural law account of basic right and wrong actions, then we can see how virtues and happiness fit in. If we are in the habit of performing actions that promote important human goods, then we have a moral virtue. Take the virtues of prudence, temperance, and fortitude as examples. Recall from section 1.4 that prudence is the trait of making good judgments, temperance is balancing the attraction of pleasures and desires and instincts, and fortitude is being determined and courageous. Are you prudent about protecting your own life (a basic good), or are you reckless and careless? Do you show temperance with regard to sex (a basic good), or are you self-indulgent? Do you show the courage to protect your neighbor's life (a basic good) when it is threatened, or do you show cowardice? Each of these virtues gets developed out of repeated actions. To develop prudence you must act prudently, to develop temperance you must act temperately, to develop courage you must act courageously. As Aquinas puts it:

if the acts be multiplied, a certain quality is formed. (1274, I-II, Q51, article 2)

and

a habit of virtue cannot be caused by one act, but only by many. (1274, I-II, Q51, article 3)

Although living in accord with the natural law and developing moral virtues can lead to a degree of happiness, the theological virtues, given to us and made known to us through sacred scripture, are necessary for "supernatural happiness." Here is how Aquinas explains how theological virtues tie into ultimate happiness. Supernatural happiness, he writes,

> is a happiness surpassing man's nature, and which man can obtain by the power of God alone ... And because such happiness surpasses the capacity of human nature, man's natural principles which enable him to act well according to his capacity, do not suffice to direct man to this same happiness. Hence it is necessary for man to receive from God some additional principles, whereby he may be directed to supernatural happiness ... Such like principles are called "theological virtues": first, because their object is God, inasmuch as they direct us aright to God: secondly, because they are infused in us by God alone: thirdly, because these virtues are not made known to us, save by Divine revelation, contained in Holy Writ. (1274, I-II, Q62, article 1)

So, again, although through reason alone we can become aware of the natural law and what it ethically requires, our "natural principles" as Aquinas calls it in the above quotation, are not enough for us to reach ultimate happiness. The natural law as an ethical standard written on the human heart is more of a moral baseline that humans have, which inclines them toward happiness. But reason alone won't get us to the ultimate end that God wants for us.

That ultimate end of supernatural happiness requires theological virtues. And, as Aquinas points out at the end of the previous long quotation, those theological virtues are only known to us through "Divine revelation"; "Holy Writ," which is the Bible; or, simply, divine law.

Where in divine law do we learn of the theological virtues? As we saw in chapter 1, they are most clearly specified in the New Testament, what Aquinas calls the *new law*. The new law differs from natural law in an important way, because "the faithful need to be instructed ... both by word and writing, both as to what they should believe and as to what they should do" (1274, I-II, Q106, article 1). Once people are exposed to the grace of the new law, which is "a written law," then it is possible for the New Law to be "inscribed on our hearts" (1274, I-II, Q106, article 1).

Charity, as we saw in section 1.4, is the greatest Christian virtue. Aquinas gives a nice argument to underscore this Christian belief. The theological virtue of charity approaches nearer to God, he argues. "Because the others, in their very nature, imply a certain distance from the object: since faith is of what is not seen, and hope is of what is not possessed" (1274, I-II, Q66, article 6).

Aquinas agrees with Augustine that the Sermon on the Mount, which is found in the New Law, "contains the whole process of forming the life of a Christian" (1274, I-II, Q108, article 3). And Aquinas pulls in the idea we saw in section 1.2 that ethics is concerned not only with our external actions, but also our internal thoughts, intentions, and motives. Aquinas calls this our "interior movements," and he discusses how Jesus teaches that we

> should refrain not merely from those external works that are evil in themselves, but also from internal acts, and from the occasions of evil deeds. In the second place He directs man's intention. (1274, I-II, Q108, article 3)

A memorable expression that Aquinas uses to capture this aspect of Christian ethics is that exterior acts belong to the hand and interior acts belong to the mind. The new law, he writes, "by restraining the mind from inordinate movements, must needs also restrain the hand from inordinate acts, which ensue from inward movements" (1274, I-II, Q108, article 1).

Before we end this section, let us revisit the just war theory, which was mentioned at the end of section 2.1 in the context of discussing Augustine's contributions to Catholic ethics. Aquinas continued the Catholic tradition's development of the just war theory (1274, II-II, Q40, article 1). Aquinas claimed that in order for a war to be just, three things are necessary: (1) The war must be declared by a legitimate political authority who has the responsibility of watching over the country. (2) The war must be waged for a just cause, for instance that "those who are attacked, should be attacked because they deserve it." And (3), it is necessary that war is waged with "a rightful intention, so that they intend the advancement of good, or the avoidance of evil." So, if a war is declared by the legitimate authority, and for a just cause, it may still be an unjust war if it is waged because of "a wicked intention."

2.3 Conclusion

In this chapter we have focused on Catholic ethics as it was refined and elaborated during the medieval era. In both Augustine and Aquinas we saw how the ancient sources of Catholic ethics—the Old Testament and New Testament—remained as the roots of the ethical tradition.

The components of Catholic ethics—its ethical concepts, ethical principles, and ethical theories—become even more well established as they continue to be reflected on by moral theologians and philosophers such as Augustine and Aquinas. We have seen that the concepts of virtue and happiness, for instance, continue to have a central place in medieval Catholic ethics. In addition to continuing the Catholic tradition of virtue ethics, Aquinas further developed the natural law concept into a fuller natural law ethical theory. We saw how Aquinas gathered many dimensions of Catholic ethics by using the categories of divine law, eternal law, human law, and natural law. With a natural law account of human actions, Aquinas was able to pull together virtues, happiness, and supernatural happiness.

Another constant theme in Catholic ethics that we saw in both Augustine and Aquinas is how ethics is viewed as rooted both in God's word as well as in human nature and human reason. So, although Aquinas holds that the theological virtues, as well as being exposed to divine law, are necessary for achieving supernatural happiness, for instance, he maintains his confidence in the agreement between faith and reason, since both the natural and eternal laws can be recognized through reason alone. And the ethical demands of the natural law are consistent with the ethical demands of the divine law.

In the next chapter we will venture into the early modern era. We will move beyond Catholic virtue ethics and natural law ethics and into yet another ethical theory, known as deontological ethics.

Concepts, Principles, Theories, and Traditions Introduced in Chapter 2

Concepts

Theology
Moral theology
Natural law
Human law
Common good

Grace
Freedom/free will
Divine law
Eternal law

Nicene Creed
Sin
Natural inclinations
Human goods

Principles

Principle of natural law

Theories

Just war theory
Natural law ethics

Traditions

Natural law ethics

Review Questions

1. What are some examples that show how Augustine continues the Catholic tradition of viewing ethics through faith and reason?
2. What are some examples that show how Aquinas continues the Catholic tradition of viewing ethics through faith and reason?
3. Which kind of law has existed longer, divine law or eternal law? Why?
4. According to Aquinas, what are some important human goods we can identify just by looking at human natural inclinations? And why do you think they are called "goods"?
5. According to Aquinas, what are the three necessary conditions for a just war?

Discussion Questions

1. Describe some of Augustine's ideas about virtue ethics. Do you yourself understand virtue as the perfect love of God? Explain.
2. What would be a specific example of when a human law came into conflict with natural law or divine law? Explain.
3. The *Catechism of the Catholic Church* says that the "natural law is immutable and permanent throughout the variations of history; it subsists under the flux of ideas and customs and supports their progress" (1992, sec 1958). Would Aquinas agree with this statement? Explain.
4. St. Paul and St. Thomas Aquinas both say that the natural law is written on the human heart. Yet in the world today we see much cultural diversity. By using the following quotation from the *Catechism of the Catholic Church*, explain how a universal natural law is consistent with an observation of cultural diversity: "Application of the natural law varies greatly ... Nevertheless, in the diversity of cultures, the natural law remains as a rule that binds men among themselves and imposes on them, beyond the inevitable differences, common principles" (1992, sec 1957).
5. Using Aquinas' just war theory, describe a just or unjust war you have learned about.

3

MODERN CATHOLIC ETHICS

3.1 Manuals of Moral Theology

During the medieval period, Catholic ethics was brought together and summarized in various *summas*. Think of the Catholic ethical tradition with all of its components we saw tied together during the medieval period as a great banquet, a great feast of ethical concepts, principles, and theories. With that in mind, consider this parable that Jesus offered:

> *A man gave a great dinner to which he invited many. When the time for the dinner came, he dispatched his servant to say to those invited, "Come, everything is now ready." But one by one, they all began to excuse themselves. The first said to him, "I have purchased a field and must go to examine it; I ask you, consider me excused." And another said, "I have purchased five yoke of oxen and am on my way to evaluate them; I ask you, consider me excused." And another said, "I have just married a woman, and therefore I cannot come." The servant went and reported this to his master. Then the master of the house in a rage commanded his servant, "Go out quickly into the streets and alleys of the town and bring in here the poor and the crippled, the blind and the lame."*

> *The servant reported, "Sir, your orders have been carried out and still there is room." (Luke 14:16–22)*

Even though the Catholic ethical tradition is a great feast that is ready for all of us, and we are invited to enjoy it, we may have other things to do and we may decide that we are not interested in enjoying the banquet.

As we now move into the modern period of the Catholic ethical tradition, we enter a period of Church history in which there was much turmoil. During the modern period between 1400 and 1900, as a remedy to help people get clear on the most important aspects of Catholic ethics, many manuals of moral theology were composed. The *Institutiones Morales* (1602), written by Juan Azor, is but one example of these works. As compared with the summaries of the medieval period, manuals such as Azor's work were meant to simplify Catholic ethics.

One specific way that the modern manuals streamlined Catholic ethics is by leaving out reference to the Sermon on the Mount. The authors of the modern manuals did not think the Sermon laid out an ethics for everyone to follow, but only an ethics for Jesus' select disciples. Also, these authors believed the Sermon was more about spirituality than ethics. A second, related change is that the modern manuals left out the concept of happiness. Both of these changes affect how the virtues get portrayed in the modern manuals and how the virtues are subsequently understood by modern theologians. We must look at these changes in more detail.

Let's say that we recognize that the Catholic ethical tradition is a great feast and we want to scale it down to a reasonably sized meal. How should we do it? One way is to look at how Aquinas attempted to tie all of Catholic ethics together with the concept of *law*. After all, if you thoroughly understand the concepts of the eternal law, the divine law, and the natural law and how all of the other ethical components hang from those three categories of law, won't that bring together all of the most important parts of Catholic ethics?

As we saw in section 1.1 when discussing the Ten Commandments, when God gives commands about what we ought to do—and that's essentially what the eternal, divine, and natural law are, right?—then that means we have a duty and obligation to carry out what the commands tell us to do. A simple way to sum up and simplify Catholic ethics, then, is to say that it lays out all our ethical *obligations*. The word *obligation* comes from the Latin word *obligare*, which means "to bind," "to connect." God's law gives us our ethical obligation; in other words, God's law is binding upon us.

With this new, modern, simplified approach for presenting Catholic ethics, we quickly notice that *happiness* gets left out. An unwavering focus on ethical obligation as our central concern tends to crowd out the idea of happiness. If something is truly an ethical obligation, then does it matter whether fulfilling the obligation will lead to your happiness or not? No, because it is part of the very meaning of an obligation that it is something you must do, something you are obligated to do, regardless of any kind of payoff there might be for fulfilling the obligation.

When the idea of happiness gets crowded out, then something else happens, too. The very meaning of the virtues gets subtly changed. In the ancient and medieval periods we saw that the virtues have a natural and logical fit with happiness; specifically, having virtues sets one on the path for attaining happiness. With this modern presentation of Catholic ethics, though, the virtues come to be seen as all other aspects of Catholic ethics are seen: as obligations required by God's law. So, instead of primarily thinking of virtues as good traits for a person to have, virtues come to be seen as duties or obligations that you are commanded to fulfil.

In section 1.4 on Christian virtues we described the differences between an action-centered ethics and a virtue-centered ethics (see diagram 1.6). There we stated that a very simple and basic way to think about ethics is to think in terms of actions that are right or wrong. We determine if the actions are right or wrong by measuring them against ethical principles, such as the Ten Commandments. By shifting our ethical focus to obligations and duties, and away from traits of persons (virtues and vices), we end up with an action-centered ethics.

When comparing action-centered ethics with virtue-centered ethics, we saw that the action-centered approach is really a subset of the virtue-centered approach. In other words, the action-centered approach does not take into account the whole picture of how actions that are repeated then become virtues or vices and then contribute to our character. The action-centered approach focuses on the action (and the intention that motivates the action, and the action's consequence), and thereby simplifies the overall ethical context. This is exactly what we said the modern manuals of moral theology were trying to do: give a simplified account of Catholic ethics. In sum, the modern manuals of moral theology simplified Catholic ethics by emphasizing obligation and deemphasizing happiness, ending up with an action-centered approach that altered the meaning and importance of the virtues.

3.2 Morality of Obligation

A simple way to capture what happened is to say that the modern manuals have reduced a rich Catholic ethics down to a simple *morality of obligation*. Or, in terms of the banquet metaphor, the manuals reduced a multicourse feast down to one simple appetizer. Ethical theories that prioritize duty and obligation as the most important dimension of ethics are known as *deontological ethical theories*. (The Greek word *deon* means "duty.") So, in simplifying Catholic ethics in this way, the modern manuals portrayed Catholic ethics as a purely deontological ethics; that is, a simple morality of obligation.

Another feature of Catholic ethics that gets emphasized by the modern manuals, because of their focus on a morality of obligation, is human freedom. Central to a morality of obligation is the assumption of human freedom. This is because to say that one has an obligation to do something logically implies that one is *capable* of doing it. If I say that you have an obligation to do something that you are incapable of doing, then how could it be binding on you? I can't reasonably say you *should* do something that you are incapable of doing.

Here is an extreme example to illustrate the point. What if I said that the oak tree growing in front of my house has an obligation not to extend its branches over my roof? I go out front and I tell the oak tree "you should not extend your branches over my roof; grow your branches in a different direction." This wouldn't make any sense. If the tree is incapable of following through with the obligation, then I can't rightly say that the tree has an obligation. Ethical theorists call this basic principle that obligations presuppose the ability to fulfil the obligation "ought implies can."

> Ought implies can: *To say you should (ought to) do something presupposes that you are capable of doing it.*

Freedom is the basic ability that the oak tree does not have but that it would need if it could fulfill obligations. In keeping with the Genesis statement that humans are made in the image and likeness of God, since God has freedom and free will, then human beings have freedom and free will, too. The Catholic tradition believes that humans have freedom, and thus it makes sense to hold humans accountable for their actions. It makes sense to say humans have obligations and duties to fulfill, and if they don't fulfill their obligations, then they are the ones responsible for choosing not to fulfill them.

Also, human beings, as *rational* creatures, are made in God's image, since God is wise and has an intelligent mind. With thinking and reasoning abilities, humans can become aware of God's law and what their obligations are. Trees, of course, lack freedom and reason, so trees cannot be said to have ethical obligations. The main point here is that central to any deontological ethics is the recognition that human beings have freedom. For the Catholic deontological ethics that the modern manuals outline, humans have the freedom to choose to obey God's law or to choose to disobey God's law. Of course, the manuals say that people *should* obey God's law, for that is the right ethical choice.

Let us now take a quick look at a few other important ethical concepts that come to be used more and more frequently during the modern and contemporary periods of the Catholic ethical tradition.

The first one is the ethical concept of a *person*. During the medieval period, Aquinas stated that individual creatures that are rational are called *persons* (1274, I, Q9, article 1). God, too, is a person. In fact, the Christian tradition holds that God is three persons in one; this is known as the *trinity*. God is Father, Son, and Holy Spirit (as the Nicene Creed explains).

Another ethical concept is *dignity*. Aquinas uses the term *dignity* to capture the sense of value that human persons have, due to their divine image (1274, III, Q4, article 1). He says

> because subsistence in a rational nature is of high dignity, therefore every individual of the rational nature is called a "person." (1274, I, Q28, article 3)

A few centuries prior to Aquinas, another Catholic theologian, St. Anselm of Canterbury, described human dignity in this way:

> to what canst thou turn thy thoughts more wholesomely and profitably than to the sweet contemplations of thy Creator's immeasurable benefits toward thee. Consider therefore the greatness and dignity that He bestowed upon thee at the beginning of thy creation; and judge for thyself with what love and reverence He ought to be worshipped. For when, as He was creating and ordering the whole world of things visible and invisible, He had determined to create the nature of man, He took high counsel concerning the <u>dignity</u> of thy condition, forasmuch as He determined to honour thee more highly than all other creatures that are in the world. (1075, Meditation I, emphasis added)

In addition to person and dignity, another ethical concept that becomes more popular during the modern and contemporary periods is the concept of *moral rights*. When Aquinas discussed the virtue of justice, he stated that "right is the object of justice" (1274, II-II, Q57, articles 1–4). In Aquinas' example, people can have "a right to something," for example, a "payment of the wage due for a service rendered." A Catholic philosopher of the early modern period, Francisco Suárez (1548–1617), worked with Aquinas' natural law theory and developed the sense of personal "rights" that we are familiar with today. In addition to saying that you have a right (such as a right to a wage) because of something you have done (such as provide a service of some kind), the modern concept of a personal "right" is a legitimate and rightful claim you have, even if you haven't done anything. This kind of personal right is acknowledged and recognized, simply because a person is made in God's image and has dignity.

During the modern and contemporary periods of the Catholic ethical tradition, the concepts *rights*, *dignity* and *person*, become more and more widely used.

3.3 Conclusion

The modern period we have been discussing in this chapter runs from 1400 to 1900. A late example of one of these manuals is a work by Massimo Massimi (1937). It is offered as an introduction and summary of the fundamental elements of Catholic ethics. Part 1 of the work contains eight chapters, and seven of the eight of them are about law. Part 2 of the work contains seven chapters, and every one of them focuses on duties. It does seem that a real danger in providing an introduction to Catholic ethics is reducing it to a purely deontological ethics, a duty-driven ethics.

Let us now turn to the contemporary period of Catholic ethics, in which we see all dimensions of Catholic ethics brought into focus. The deontological strands of Catholic ethics are important and essential, but so, too, are the virtue and natural law strands of Catholic ethics.

Concepts, Principles, Theories, and Traditions Introduced in Chapter 3

Concepts

Obligation
Freedom
Dignity

Person
Trinity
Moral rights

Principles

Ought implies can

Theories

Deontological ethics (morality of obligation)

Traditions

Deontological ethics

Review Questions

1. In their quest to provide a simplified account of Catholic ethics, what are some things that the modern manuals of moral theology left out?
2. According to the modern manuals of moral theology, where do our ethical obligations come from? Explain.
3. How does a focus on obligation crowd out the concept of happiness? Explain.
4. Explain how a focus on obligation can change how we understand what a virtue is.
5. Is deontological ethics an action-centered ethics or a virtue-centered ethics? Explain the difference.
6. Explain how freedom is an important background assumption of a deontological ethics.

Discussion Questions

1. We have seen the ways in which the modern manuals of moral theology attempted to simplify Catholic ethics. If you were given the task of simplifying Catholic ethics, how would you do it? Would you do it differently than the authors of the manuals did it? Why or why not? Explain.

2. The *Catechism of the Catholic Church* says: "To choose deliberately— that is, both knowing it and willing it—something gravely contrary to the divine law and to the ultimate end of man is to commit a mortal sin. This destroys in us the charity without which eternal beatitude is impossible. Unrepented, it brings eternal death" (1992, sec 1874). Explain how deontological ethics and the principle *ought implies can* applies to the Church's position on mortal sin.

3. An ancient Roman proverb says: "Do justice, and let the skies fall." Explain how this fits with deontological ethics. In your answer, use the concepts of duty, obligation, and happiness.

4. In the Parable of the Lost Son, also known as the Prodigal Son (Luke 15:11–32), Jesus describes the relationship between a father and his two sons. The younger son asked his father for his share of his inheritance. The father gave it to him and his son set off to a distant country. He wastefully spends his entire inheritance (he is prodigal with his money). When he is penniless, he takes a job at a farm tending to pigs. He is so hungry that he is half-inclined to eat the pigs' food. It occurs to him that his father's hired workers have plenty of food. He decides to go back to his father, confess he was wrong, and ask to be treated as a hired worker. When the son returns, the father, filled with compassion, embraced and kissed his son. The father decided to celebrate the return of his son with a feast. The older son, who was working in the field, was surprised to find the celebration. In anger, he said to his father, "I have served you for years and yet when your irresponsible son returns, you lavish him with a feast!" But the father responded: "we must celebrate because your brother was lost and has been found." Explain how the older brother's reaction illustrates a deontological ethics and the father's reaction illustrates virtue ethics.

4

CONTEMPORARY CATHOLIC ETHICS

I n one of his parables, Jesus talked of a very small kind of seed, a
mustard seed. Interpreters of Jesus' parable of the mustard seed
say that Jesus is basically talking about the growth of the Church.

> The kingdom of heaven is like a grain of mustard seed that
> a person took and sowed in a field. It is the smallest of all
> the seeds, yet when full-grown it is the largest of plants. It
> becomes a large bush, and the birds of the sky come and dwell
> in its branches. (Matthew 13:31–32)

The Church had its origin in humble beginnings of the ancient
world and has endured for twenty-one centuries. The Church
began as a tiny seed and is now a large tree with many branches.

4.1 Catholic Social Teaching: Issues

The Catholic tradition has always had an interest in society and the
rules and laws for social living. But in the late nineteenth century
a specific moral teaching concerning economics and the structure
of society began to develop in the Catholic tradition. During this
time period, large changes were taking place in societies and in civi-
lization generally, changes that were affecting people's day-to-day

lives. In response to historical events such as the Industrial Revolution, the Catholic Church began to formulate a specific Catholic social teaching.

Catholic social teaching is an ethical teaching that suggests criteria for moral reflection, for moral judgment, and guidelines for action. As free beings with a capacity for reason, human beings have choices about how they will live and which practices of society they will follow. Catholic social teaching as we know it today was formed over time (see diagram 4.1). The focus of Catholic social teaching is always the human person in society. With a sense of continuous renewal, Catholic social teaching is meant to help guide Christians in how to deal with new social issues as they arise. Catholic social teaching draws from and builds on ethical components from the long Catholic ethical tradition—ethical concepts and principles from the Bible as well as from later developments.

Diagram 4.1

	Important Sources of Catholic Social Teaching
1891	*Rerum Novarum*, by Pope Leo XIII
1931	*Quadragesimo Anno*, by Pope Pius XI
1963	*Pacem in Terris*, by Pope John XXIII
1965	*Gaudium et Spes*, publication of the Second Vatican Council
1965	*Dignitatis Humanae*, publication of the Second Vatican Council
1967	*Populorum Progressio*, by Pope Paul VI
1971	*Octogesima Adveniens*, by Pope Paul VI
1981	*Laborem Exercens*, by Pope John Paul II
1987	*Sollicitudo Rei Socialis*, by Pope John Paul II
1991	*Centesimus Annus*, by Pope John Paul II
2009	*Caritas in Veritate*, by Pope Benedict XVI

In the nineteenth century the Industrial Revolution was an important shift that took place in society: products that were traditionally made by hand (through manual labor), now, because of organizational, economic, and technological developments, were able to be produced by machines, in large factories. People experienced new forms of work, new forms of ownership, new and different business practices, as well as different social, political, and economic experiments, such as totalitarianism, communism, and socialism.

Aware of these enormous events taking place in society, the Church responded by formulating positions on specific social, political, and economic topics. Pope Leo XIII is credited with initiating the development of contemporary Catholic social teaching with the publication of his work entitled *Rerum Novarum* (1891), which in Latin means "Of New Things." In that work Pope Leo discussed the condition of workers during the late 1800s—their wages, the number of hours they were required to work, health and safety standards in the workplace, child labor, worker associations—basically, the overall working conditions of the time.

Pope Leo pointed out that new systems in society were responsible for both the creation of great wealth and yet, at the same time, large numbers of poor workers. Pope Leo defended private property, and so he argued against socialism, which was a system that some theorists at the time had suggested as a way to deal with the imbalance between rich and poor.

In 1931, on the fortieth anniversary of the publication of *Rerum Novarum*, Pope Pius XI published the work *Quadragesimo Anno*, which in Latin means "Fortieth Year." In this work, Pope Pius XI praised Pope Leo's *Rerum Novarum* and expressed how important and appropriate it was in addressing social concerns. Pope Pius XI restated many of Pope Leo's points about private property; the condition of workers, including their wages, their associations, and workplace conditions; and applied what Leo said in 1891 to society in 1931. Although many workers' conditions were improved by then, Pius said, there was still a great gap between nonowning workers and the very rich. Pius also argued that neither socialism nor communism is consistent with ethical teachings that derive from the Bible.

In 1963, Pope John XXIII published *Pacem in Terris* (Latin for "Peace on Earth"), in which he discussed how the world now consisted of many independent nations, each with its own government and constitution. Pope John also discussed how citizens relate to their governments, including minority citizens. He discussed political communities and the United Nations (UN), which was established in 1945.

Pope John noted that the interdependence of national economies had grown deeper, and that while some nations were highly developed, others were still in the process of developing. Another serious dimension of the social and political climate of the time was brought about by various new technologies. Weapons technologies had become highly advanced, including the invention of nuclear weapons. John XXIII discussed the arms race that was occurring at the time, and how nations were stockpiling these weapons.

Pope Paul VI had two publications that contributed to Catholic social teaching: *Populorum Progressio* (Latin for "The Development of Peoples") (1967) and *Octogesima Adveniens* (Latin for "Eightieth Anniversary") (1971).

In *Populorum Progressio* Paul VI discussed the poor people of the world, especially those in developing countries facing disease, hunger for food, and hunger for education. Authentic human development, he wrote, is not only about economic growth, but it is a fuller human development, one in which the full range of human needs can be fulfilled. He discussed how work, profit, and competition relate to economic progress and successful human development. And he addressed the excessive economic and social inequalities between rich countries and poor nations.

In *Octogesima Adveniens* Paul VI celebrated the eightieth anniversary of the publication of *Rerum Novarum*, and he continued to address the inequalities between nations. Urbanization was a new social issue, he claimed, since city centers with intense concentration of population could lead to dehumanizing living conditions. Paul VI also pointed to exploitation of nature and negative impact on the environment. And in discussing the importance and impact of economics and politics on the world, he said the world had become dominated by scientific and technological change.

Pope John Paul II had several publications that contributed to Catholic social teaching. First was his *Laborem Exercens* ("Human Work"), which was published in 1981, on the ninetieth anniversary of *Rerum Novarum*. In this document John Paul II provided a theoretical analysis of all kinds of human activity, ranging from manual work to intellectual work, including white-collar work. John Paul II described new developments in technological, economic, and political conditions, such as automated production, increases in the cost of energy, and more pollution of nature, which were influencing the world of work. He discussed how work has economic dimensions and is also a foundation for family life.

In his *Sollicitudo Rei Socialis* ("Social Concern") (1987), which was published on the twentieth anniversary of Paul VI's *Populorum Progressio*, John Paul II discussed the continuing problem of the development and underdevelopment of peoples and the obstacles that stand in the way of authentic human development. The issue is that the developing countries are more numerous than the developed countries. And this means that the people who lack the benefits of development are more numerous than those who possess these benefits. The world's resources, he stated, are unequally distributed. Some people have an excessive availability of material goods and engage in consumerism, whereas others are suffering from underdevelopment.

John Paul II's document *Centesimus Annus* ("Hundredth Anniversary") (1991) celebrated the hundredth anniversary of the publication of *Rerum Novarum*. In this work John Paul II described how in the 1980s dictatorships in Latin America, Africa, and Asia collapsed, and in 1989 countries in eastern and central Europe abandoned communism. Much rebuilding was then needed in those countries. He discussed property, material goods, land, natural resources, and ownership. Another form of ownership that he said is important is possession of know-how, technology, and skill. There are many poor countries that lack these resources, but, in addition, are in debt to richer countries. John Paul II also discussed capitalism, free markets, business, profit, and monopolies, and the government's role. A discussion of the appropriate tasks of law and government led him to look at democracy, totalitarianism, and fundamentalism. He wrote about the use of drugs, the destruction of the natural environment to feed consumerism, war, and globalization.

Pope Benedict XVI has also contributed to Catholic social teaching, with his *Caritas in Veritate* ("Charity in Truth") (2009). Following his predecessors, he deals further with the topic of globalization and authentic human development. Although there has been technological and economic development and progress, world hunger and food insecurity still exist, he says; it is thus still necessary for Pope Benedict to carefully examine commercial relationships and economic activity. He discusses many aspects of economic life: business activity, the different stakeholders involved, and different types of businesses, including the world of finance. In addition, Pope Benedict addresses population growth, nonrenewable energy sources, and humanity's relationship to the natural environment.

4.2 Catholic Social Teaching: Ethics

Now that we have a rough outline of the issues addressed by contemporary Catholic social teaching, we will examine how various popes have applied to these issues the many ethical components from the long Catholic ethical tradition.

But before we get into the ethical specifics, we should review a point that was made in section 1.1 of chapter 1. There is an important difference between *ethical* statements, which are about what we *should* do, and other kinds of statements—ones that only describe the world and the things in the world. In section 4.1, the focus was looking at events that were happening in the world from the late 1800s to very recent times. Most of section 4.1 was simply *describing* these historical events. To only describe historical events is not to make *ethical* statements about them. If we wish to make *ethical* statements about these various events, then we will have to use *ethical* concepts and principles. And that is exactly what we find in the Catholic social teaching documents. In reaching conclusions about various social issues, the popes use virtue ethics concepts, natural law concepts, deontological concepts, and make reference to both the Old and New Testament parts of the Bible (see appendix 2).

For instance, starting with the influential document *Rerum Novarum*, Pope Leo stated he was using "principles of Christian living as found in the Gospel." About employers and employees, he pointed out that each has particular rights to which they are entitled, as well as duties that are required of them. The right to private ownership, he said, was in accordance with natural law. Also, *just* human laws regarding work and working conditions derive their binding force from natural law and divine law. He related these issues to commandments nine and ten, about coveting. And he used the language of virtues and vices. The vices of avarice, envy, pride, and injustice are relevant to the issues, as well as the virtues of justice, thrift, prudence, mercy, and charity.

Forty years later, when Pope Pius XI revisited the issues in his *Quadragesimo Anno*, he, too, referred to the Bible and the Gospel, and applied various ethical concepts. He described how God has created human beings with a social nature, to live in society, and that by faithfully fulfilling duties people can achieve happiness, in this life, and eternal happiness. He critiqued socialism, because socialism requires that people surrender themselves entirely to society, and sacrifice their liberty for the socialist model of producing goods. This, he said, is damaging to human dignity. He made the case that socialism is out of keeping with the natural moral law, and that natural and divine law are guiding lights to meet the needs of the common good. He focused on the virtue of justice and its associated vice, injustice.

See appendix 2 for how the other popes applied ethical concepts to contemporary issues.

4.3 Catechism of 1992

In the Church's twentieth century, limitations were identified with the modern manuals of moral theology that we discussed in chapter 3. In 1962 a very large meeting was organized by the Catholic Church with the aim of renewing the life of the Church. This meeting is known as the Second Vatican Council, and it took place from 1962 to 1965. In the history of the Church there have been many councils (a total of 21). In chapter 2, for example, we mentioned the Council of Nicaea that took place in the year 325. The Second Vatican Council was the second time that a meeting like this took place in Vatican City in Rome. The First Vatican Council took place in the nineteenth century, during the years 1859 to 1870.

Out of the reflections at the Second Vatican Council, the Catholic bishops realized that a new *Catechism of the Catholic Church* (CCC) could contribute to the renewal of the life of the Church. The word *catechism* comes from a Greek word that means "to teach orally." The last time a catechism of the entirety of Catholic teaching was created was 1566; it was published a few years after the Council of Trent (1545–1563). The catechism that was published in 1566 is known as the *Catechism of the Council of Trent*, or the *Roman Catechism*.

In 1992, the Catholic Church published a new and more comprehensive *Catholic Catechism*, in which it sought to present the entirety of Catholic teaching in terms of faith and ethics. The *Catechism* has four parts. The first part discusses the Profession of Faith (see diagram 2.1). The second part discusses the seven sacraments. The third part discusses ethics (it is called "Life in Christ"). And the fourth part discusses Christian prayer, especially The Lord's Prayer (the "Our Father").

So what kind of ethics do we find in part three of the *Catechism?* Here are some ethical concepts you will find in the *Catechism:* virtue, duty, natural law, moral rights, moral command, and happiness (see diagram 4.2).

Diagram 4.2

Ethical Concepts in the *Catechism* (1992)	
Virtue	"The most important virtue is charity" (sec 1826).
Duty	"The Ten Commandments express our fundamental duties toward God and neighbor" (sec 2072).
Natural law	"The natural law expresses the original moral sense which enables us to discern by reason the good and the evil" (sec 1954).
Moral rights	"The natural law, present in the heart of each person, expresses the dignity of the person and determines the basis for fundamental rights and duties" (secs 1956, 1978).
Moral command	"The Ten Commandments must be interpreted in light of Jesus' twofold yet single commandment of love: "love God with all your heart and love your neighbor as yourself" (sec 2055).
Happiness	"True happiness and eternal happiness are found in God" (secs 1723, 1863).

Some ethical principles found in the *Catechism* include the principle of the Golden Rule, the Pauline principle, and the principle of charity (see diagram 4.3). The *Catechism* says that these ethical principles apply in every case.

Now let's try to bring the ethical pieces together. The *Catechism* explains that the Ten Commandments must be interpreted in the light of Jesus' twofold yet single commandment of love: love God with all your heart and love your neighbor as yourself. Charity is the theological virtue of love. The practice of all the virtues is animated and inspired by charity. Since the New Testament, we have seen how charity is a special virtue, not only because it is most important, but in how it is acquired.

Diagram 4.3

Ethical Principles in the *Catechism* (1992)	
Principle of the Golden Rule	"Whatever you wish that men would do to you, do so to them" (sec 1789).
Pauline principle	"One may never do evil so that good will result from it" (sec 1789).
Principle of charity	"Love God with all your heart and love your neighbor as yourself" (sec 1789).

The virtue of charity, along with the virtues faith and hope, are infused by God into human souls. And charity, faith, and hope are three theological virtues that most directly correspond to the first three commandments, which are about our personal relationship with God (see diagram 4.4). The other seven commandments are about how we deal with other people, and we can see how many moral virtues are relevant in our dealings with others. With this diagram we can also see that the essential duties we have from the Ten

Diagram 4.4

Jesus' Twofold Commandment of Love (Principle of Charity)	
LOVE **God with all your heart.**	1. I am the Lord your God.
	2. You shall not take the name of the Lord in vain.
Faith & Hope	3. Remember to keep holy the Lord's Day.
LOVE **your neighbor as yourself.**	4. Honor your father and your mother.
	5. You shall not kill.
Gratitude, Chastity	6. You shall not commit adultery.
Justice	7. You shall not steal.
Temperance	8. You shall not bear false witness.
Truthfulness	9. You shall not covet your neighbor's wife.
Patience Humility	10. You shall not covet your neighbor's goods.

Commandments have their place as well. One last item of note about the new *Catechism* is that Catholic social teaching also is included. The *Catechism* discusses each of the Ten Commandments, one by one, and explains the duties involved and the relevant virtues. And, where appropriate, we see Catholic social teaching spelled out in the *Catechism* also. In the discussion of the seventh commandment, you shall not steal, for instance (secs 2401–2463), the *Catechism* sums up the main elements of Catholic social teaching.

4.4 Compendium of 2005

Although Catholic social teaching is included in the *Catechism*, Pope John Paul II expressed interest in another more extensive document that would pull together all ethical teachings of the Church. So the Pontifical Council of the Church went to work, and in 2005 published a *Compendium of Catholic Social Teaching*. The *Compendium* is a work that offers a comprehensive collection of Catholic ethical teachings.

In its introduction the *Compendium* describes how the Catholic Church is interested in ethical and philosophical questions about human society and humanity's place in nature. The *Compendium* then spells out how the Church has answered these questions with its social teachings. In effect, the *Compendium* summarizes over one hundred years of reflection on the development of Catholic social teaching (from the years 1891 to 2005).

The *Compendium* takes the ethical concepts and principles we have been looking at, and by drawing on various Church documents from the last hundred years, then applies them to a wide variety of topics. The ethical concepts touched on include the Ten Commandments, Jesus as a model, virtues, the Golden Rule, faith, reason, natural law, dignity, duties, rights, and the common good.

In the *Compendium*, there are chapters on the human person and God's plan for humanity, then chapters on human rights, property, the family, human work, economic life, political communities, the international community, peace, and the natural environment.

The *Compendium* goes beyond the basic ethical concepts and principles and the social issues we have looked at. It boils down Catholic social teaching to its essence and sums up Catholic social teaching with a set of summary principles meant to capture the ethical foundations of a century of Catholic social teaching (see diagram 4.5). These summary principles range from the dignity of human persons due to their being made in the image and likeness of God to more specific ethical principles concerning the common good, the poor, and life in a political community. We will look at some of these principles in more detail in later chapters of *CFE*.

Diagram 4.5

Principles of Catholic Social Teaching in the *Compendium* (2005)	
Personalist principle	The human person is made in the image of God and has dignity (secs 107–159).
Principle of the common good	There is a common good that humanity is responsible for ensuring and attaining (secs 160–184).
Principle of the universal destination of goods	God destined the earth and all it contains for all peoples (secs 171–184).
Principle of the preferential option for the poor	The poor and marginalized should be the focus of particular concern (secs 182–184).
Principle of subsidiarity	A larger organization should help and allow subordinate organizations to achieve those tasks of which they are capable, without interference (secs 185–188).
Principle of participation	Citizens should participate and contribute to the common good, through political participation (secs 189–191).
Principle of solidarity	We must be determined to commit ourselves in solidarity to the good of all (secs 193–196).

4.5 Conclusion

In section 4.1, we sketched the economic, social, and political issues addressed with Catholic social teaching. Then, in section 4.2 we went through some of those same issues, incorporating the ethical components of previous chapters, and explained how those ethical components feed into these particular social teachings. After that, we reviewed the main ethical components that are used in the two important contemporary documents of the Catholic ethical tradition, the *Catechism* of 1992 and the *Compendium* of 2005. Now that we have taken the Catholic ethical tradition in view—as it spans from the ancient, medieval, modern, and contemporary periods—we will turn to the Franciscan ethical tradition, which is a small part of the Catholic ethical tradition. As mentioned in the Introduction to *CFE*, the Franciscan tradition began with the life, teachings, and ethical and spiritual insights of St. Francis of Assisi (1181–1226), who lived in the medieval period of Catholic history. It is to the life of St. Francis that we will now turn.

Concepts, Principles, Theories, and Traditions Introduced in Chapter 4

Concepts

Catechism
Compendium
Second Vatican Council

Principles

Personalist principle
Principle of the common good
Principle of the universal destination of goods
Principle of the preferential option for the poor

Principle of subsidiarity
Principle of participation
Principle of solidarity

Traditions

Catholic social teaching

Review Questions

1. What changes took place in society during the late nineteenth century that provoked the Catholic tradition to develop its social teachings?
2. According to the chapter, what kinds of ethical concepts did Pope Leo use in his influential document *Rerum Novarum* (1891)?
3. According to the chapter, what has Pope Benedict XVI contributed to Catholic social teaching?
4. Explain how the principle of charity relates to the Ten Commandments.
5. Explain how the virtues of justice and truthfulness relate to the Ten Commandments.
6. By using Catholic ethical concepts, explain what the principle of the preferential option for the poor asks us to do.

Discussion Questions

1. Pope John Paul II linked solidarity to charity (1987, para 40). He cited a passage from the Gospel of John about how to link them. Study the following passage from John's Gospel, and explain the link between solidarity and charity: "A new commandment I give unto you: That you love one another, as I have loved you, that you also love one another. By this shall all men know that you are my disciplines, if you have love one for another" (John 13:35).

2. The term *solidarity* as an ethical term may seem foreign sounding to you. As a way to get to the ethical meaning of solidarity, first think of the word *solidarity* in physical terms. The root of the word is *solid*, which is a kind of matter. Think of ice as a solid. What happens to ice when exposed to temperatures higher than 32 degrees Fahrenheit? It changes from a solid to a liquid. And what happens to this liquid when exposed to temperatures higher than thirty-two degrees? It will begin to *evaporate*; that is, it will turn to vapor, a gas. When in a solid state, the chemical bonds of water molecules are strong enough to hold molecules tightly together. In their liquid or gaseous state, water molecules are more loosely held together. Given question one above, what kind of bonds are required for the *ethical* meaning of solidarity?

3. Look at appendix 2, focus on one document from one pope, choose one issue and the ethical components listed, and try to formulate a Catholic ethical position on that issue.

4. Study the following passage from the *Catechism*, and with ethical concepts and principles, explain why the Church would take this position: "Any system in which social relationships are determined entirely by economic factors is contrary to the nature of the human person and his acts" (sec 2423).

5. The beginning of this chapter makes a comparison between Jesus' parable of the mustard seed and the growth of the Catholic Church. One image used is how the mustard seed will grow into a large bush with many branches. Think of the many Catholic organizations in existence today, such as Catholic hospitals and Catholic universities. Continuing with the analogy of the Church as a large tree with many branches, try to estimate how many people today "dwell in these branches" of the Church. Explain how you arrived at your estimate.

5

CATHOLIC FRANCISCAN ETHICS

5.1 St. Francis of Assisi

In the year 1223, when St. Francis of Assisi was forty-two years of age, he decided to celebrate the birth of Jesus in a unique way. In the town of Greccio, located in central Italy, about sixty miles south of Assisi, Francis arranged for a manger to be set up, with hay and animals gathered around it. A manger is something one finds in a stable; it is a box that holds food for the animals to eat from. After Jesus was born, his mother Mary wrapped him and put him a manger, since Mary and Joseph were staying in a stable. Francis wished to reenact the birth of Jesus that took place in Bethlehem twelve centuries earlier. In the dark on Christmas Eve, with a baby in the manger that was filled with hay, with an ox and a donkey standing by, and candles and torches to light up the night, Francis and the people of Greccio saw with their own eyes how Jesus was born into humble and poor conditions. This kind of reenactment also became known as the nativity scene, from the Latin word *nativus*, which means "birth/born."

What does this story have to do with ethics? First, we can see it as an illustration of the virtue of *humility*. For Francis, that God became human and was born into the world as an innocent and gentle child in poor and humble conditions was very profound. The theological concept *incarnation* means God took the form of human flesh in the human person of Jesus. Following Francis, the Franciscan tradition commonly refers to the *humility of the incarnation* (Thomas of Celano 1229, Book I, chp 30).

Thomas of Celano wrote the first biography of Francis, and said of Francis:

> *His highest aim, foremost desire, and greatest intention was to pay heed to the holy gospel in all things and through all things, to follow the teaching of our Lord Jesus Christ and to retrace His footsteps completely.* (1229, Book I, chapter 30)

Thomas is actually paraphrasing Francis, who, in an early writing of his own, said that he wished to "follow the teaching and footprints of our Lord Jesus Christ" (Francis 1221, chp 1).

Another related ethical concept illustrated in Francis' nativity scene is the concept of *role model*. As a Christian, Francis took Jesus as his most important role model, and aspired to achieve the virtues that Jesus taught and modeled in his lifetime. Moreover, Francis advised his brothers to "preach by their deeds" (1221, chp 17), and so Francis was familiar with the notion of modeling. In Francis, we are obviously seeing someone who sought to live a life of Christian virtue ethics. Francis became firmly convinced that following Jesus' teachings and putting Jesus' ethic into action is the way to build one's life on solid rock. Francis saw himself as a member of the Catholic tradition.

Another significant event in Francis' life that has important ethical dimensions was his first meeting with a leper. Francis had grown up in privileged circumstances because his father was a very successful cloth merchant. Francis' father hoped that Francis would take over the family business. But Francis did not see that as the right kind of life for him. After a great amount of soul searching, and a series of religious experiences, Francis became determined to follow the will of God and the teachings of Jesus. One day when he was riding his horse and saw a man with leprosy (a disease caused by bacteria, which severely damages one's skin and nerves) Francis was filled with fear and horror at the sight of the leper. But because Francis wished to stay true to his commitment to follow the will of God, he dismounted from his horse to meet the leper. The leper reached out his hand to ask for alms. Francis kissed the leper and gave him money (Bonaventure 1261, chp 1).

This story fits very well with Jesus' compassionate attitude toward people with leprosy (Matthew 8:1–4; Luke 5:12–16). It also fits with the Parable of the Good Samaritan. Consistent with the teachings of Jesus, Francis was trying to be a good Samaritan and help those in need. And Francis viewed the leper as a human person who is made in the image and likeness of God, which is a basic belief about human persons, rooted in Genesis. As we saw in the previous chapter, in the Catholic tradition this belief about persons has come to be called the *personalist principle*, which says the human person is made in the image of God and has dignity that ought to be respected.

As someone participating in the Catholic ethical tradition, Francis was living out Jesus' twofold commandment of love, which we have called the *principle of charity*—we should love God and love our neighbor as we love ourselves. And in his writings, Francis explicitly states that we should commit ourselves to Jesus' *principle of the Golden Rule* (1221, chp 4). Further, as we have seen in the previous chapter, in the Catholic tradition the principle about attending to those who are especially in need—such as lepers—has come to be called the *principle of the preferential option for the poor*.

Francis was not a trained theologian or philosopher; he never took classes at any college or university, so he was not familiar with philosophy and theology as subjects taught in universities. He became acquainted with Catholic teachings through his Church and the Bible. About the brothers who wished to join Francis in his ministry, he said: "Let all the brothers be, live, and speak as Catholics" (1221, chp 19). Both Catholic teachings and his own personal spiritual insights and experiences prompted him to become aware of the poor who were present in his society, and he became dedicated to serving those in his society whom he believed were most in need.

5.2 Franciscan Virtue Ethics

In Francis' approach to ethics, we have already seen particular virtues such as *humility*, *compassion*, and *charity*, and we have also seen the important virtue ethics concept of *role model*.

Let us look at some other virtue ethics aspects of Francis' ethical approach. In looking at the events in the life of Francis we notice that coming to an awareness of God's presence took time for Francis. In fact, developing Christian attitudes and behaviors took Francis a lifetime to develop. Also, we know from virtue ethics theory that actions can initially be difficult for us to perform, but when they are repeatedly performed they can become second nature to us (this is true of good habits and bad habits). Virtue ethics theory then says that when the habit becomes ingrained, it becomes part of one's character. Francis is an example of someone who struggled to develop virtuous traits. His character development took a lifetime. He was initially filled with fear and horror at the sight of a leper and found it difficult to treat the leper as he would treat any other person. But with faith in the teachings of Jesus he managed to overcome his fear and eventually became someone who routinely interacted with lepers and sought to attend to their needs.

Another aspect of Christian virtue ethics is apparent in Francis' commitment to the Beatitudes (Francis 1221, chp 16). As mentioned in chapter 1, the Beatitudes are the heart of Jesus's preaching since they sum up what a blessed and happy life is like. With the Beatitudes, Jesus answers the traditional philosophical question, what is true happiness? As we've seen, the Beatitudes offer ethical guidance; they tell us to be someone who is meek, merciful, pure in heart, and a peacemaker; and these do seem to be the virtues that Francis tried to develop in himself. In addition to the Christian virtues of faith, hope, charity, courage, temperance, prudence, and justice, Francis also emphasizes the virtues of humility, compassion, peacefulness, kindness, gentleness, mercy, forgiveness, generosity, modesty, and respect (Francis 1223, chp 102). And many of these virtues, such as humility, peacefulness, mercy, and forgiveness, are apparent in the Beatitudes.

The last Beatitude says "Blessed are you when men ... persecute you ... Rejoice and be glad for your reward is great in heaven." This is a very important theme in Christian ethics that Francis wholeheartedly embraces. Even when we are suffering, we have reason to rejoice and be glad. This is a point "revealed so clearly by Francis: that ... out of the most enormous physical, spiritual, emotional, or existential suffering can be born perfect joy" (Dennis et al. 1993, 152–153).

Francis did not fear death. For Francis, death was a passage into the fullness of life with Christ. He even accepted death as a "sister" who opens the way to a new life. In 1225 Francis wrote a poem called "Canticle of the Creatures" in which he praises God and God's creation. In the poem he refers to all God's creatures—living and nonliving—as brothers and sisters. In the poem, this is what Francis writes about death.

> Praised are you, my Lord, for our sister bodily Death, from whom no living man can escape. Woe on those who will die in mortal sin! Blessed are they who will be found in your most holy will, for the second death will not harm them. (1225, see appendix 3 for the full poem)

In the *Catholic Catechism* published in 1992 there is a section that discusses the meaning of Christian death as it is described in the Nicene Creed (sec 1014). In that section, the *Catechism* quotes the above stanza about death from Francis' poem.

One reason that death is not something to be feared is that, as Jesus states in the Beatitudes, true happiness is found in God. True happiness has to do with eternal life. For Francis, and for Augustine, and for Christians in the New Testament, happiness is understood as joy. In Augustine's book *The Confessions* he says that happiness is the joy in loving God (397, Book X, 22, 32). The concepts of *joy* and *rejoice* appear frequently in the New Testament. In the Christian tradition, happiness is not understood as physical pleasure; it is understood as spiritual joy. Joy is interior; it has to do with the spirit. Whereas physical pleasure is contrasted with physical pain, joy is not contrasted with pain. As Jesus teaches in the Beatitudes, even through pain and suffering we can experience spiritual blessedness, happiness, and joy. Jesus said to rejoice, and Paul and Augustine echoed Jesus' point. As a follower of Jesus, Francis, too, thought the most appropriate attitude toward life was to rejoice. According to Francis' first biographer, Thomas of Celano, Francis was firmly committed to the importance of "spiritual joy" (1247, Book II, chp 88).

Another significant event in the life of Francis that has important ethical dimensions occurred in the year 1219. That was the year Francis and a group of his followers traveled to the Middle East on a thirteen hundred–mile pilgrimage for peace. At the end of his long journey, Francis met with Sultan Malek al-Kamil, an Islamic leader. During that time period the relations between Christians and Muslims were very tense, yet Francis—true to Jesus' teachings—thought it important to love one's enemies, not hate them. Francis wrote:

> *All my brothers: let us pay attention to what the Lord says:* Love your enemies and do good to those who hate you *for our Lord Jesus Christ, Whose footprints we must follow, called His betrayer a friend and willingly offered Himself to His executioners.* (1221, chp 22)

One commentator has written that with this trip Francis "desired to share his faith not only in the Trinity and in Jesus as Saviour, but also in the universal reconciliation of all humankind and creation based on the Gospel way of life" (McMichael 2012, 136). In Francis' taking of a trip to the Middle East on a pilgrimage for peace, we can see his commitment to many Christian virtues, such as faith, hope, charity, and courage, but also the virtues of humility, compassion, peacefulness, kindness, gentleness, mercy, forgiveness, and respect.

Taking such a long journey during a time of conflict between Christians and Muslims was also very dangerous, yet Francis did not fear death. He knew he could lose his life in taking a hazardous trip, but as we heard from his biographer Thomas of Celano, Francis aimed to completely follow Jesus' teachings in all that he did.

5.3 Relational Love: Bonaventure

Francis' ethical and spiritual vision was carried forward not only by biographers such as Thomas of Celano, but also by theologians and philosophers (see diagram 5.1).

We will now look at how two medieval philosophers in particular, Bonaventure (1217–1274) and Scotus (1266–1308), sought to crystallize Francis' insights into theological and philosophical teachings that could be taught in universities and how Bonaventure and Scotus helped to contribute to the development of the Catholic ethical tradition. Historically, Franciscans have "select[ed] both Bonaventure and John Duns Scotus as the center of their Intellectual Tradition" (Osborne 2003, 2).

Bonaventure is a unique Franciscan because he was both a theologian and a philosopher, and he also wrote a biography about Francis (1261). In addition, Bonaventure was the head of the Franciscan order of friars from 1257 to 1274. Francis' small group of twelve Franciscan brothers that had formed in the year 1208 had grown to thirty thousand Franciscan friars by the year 1250!

As a Christian philosopher and theologian, Bonaventure held that the world was created by God and that in addition to being the creator, God is love, and God is a Trinity, three persons in one.

Diagram 5.1

Some Famous Franciscans	
St. Francis of Assisi	1181–1226
St. Clare of Assisi	1193–1253
Alexander of Hales	1185–1245
Anthony of Padua	1195–1231
St. Bonaventure	1217–1274
Roger Bacon	1219–1294
John Duns Scotus	1266–1308
William of Ockham	1288–1348

In Bonaventure's ethical writings, he discusses guidelines for how we should live, guidelines about right and wrong. His ethical views are informed by both the Old and the New Testaments. For example, he published a work called *Collations on the Ten Commandments* (1267), in which he examines each of the Ten Commandments from the Old Testament's book of Exodus. Bonaventure begins the work with a quotation from the Gospel of Matthew. When a young man asked Jesus how he could "gain eternal life," Jesus replied:

> If you wish to enter into life, keep the commandments. (*Matthew 19:17; quoted in Bonaventure 1267, 19*)

For Bonaventure, we should be motivated to follow the Ten Commandments because Jesus told us to do so, and because they are beneficial to us (1267, 27). Bonaventure reviews how the first three commandments concern how we should behave toward God, and the last seven address how we should behave toward our neighbor (1267, 26). Bonaventure also points out how the Ten Commandments are related to the Golden Rule and the natural law (1267, 27). Whereas it is commonly thought that the Ten Commandments were conveyed to us by God, Bonaventure tells us that, since God is three persons in one, "It is the whole Trinity that says these words" (1267, 34). In the Franciscan tradition, special emphasis is often given to remind us that God is "Three and One" and "the Creator of all things" (1267, 33).

In chapter 1 we saw that many of the Ten Commandments are explicitly about actions (e.g., about killing, stealing, adultery), and some of them are about our intentions (e.g., coveting our neighbor's goods or wife), and that Jesus in his Sermon on the Mount explained how all of the Ten Commandments can be seen as having to do with our inner intentions, thoughts, and desires. And in chapter 2 we saw how Aquinas continued this idea that ethics has to do with our external actions as well as inner thoughts, motives, and actions. Bonaventure, in this same tradition, in a work called *On the Perfection of Life*, describes how we can achieve happiness if we follow God's law "externally" as well as "interiorly" (1260, 209). Also recall from chapter 1 that a "perfection" is an ancient term for *virtue*. Thus, in this short text Bonaventure discusses how happiness—understood as joy—can be attained if we possess virtues such as humility, perseverance, and love.

As I just mentioned, Franciscans put special emphasis on God as Trinity. The Trinity is three persons in one; it is a community of relationships. In brief, Franciscans view God as *relational*. Since God is relational, it is not surprising that the natural world that was created by God is also relational.

The natural world is not simply a large collection of objects—those objects are in relation with each other. The sciences, as they came to be more and more developed in the nineteenth and twentieth centuries, also came to see the natural world as relational. Think of sciences such as physics, biology, ecology, and sociology.

Also, in the Christian view, God is love, and the three persons in the Trinity participate in a relationship of love; so, too, then, should the beings in the natural world participate in a relationship of love. In this way, a Trinitarian view of God harmonizes with the *ethical principle of charity*.

While these ideas may seem very theoretical and theological, a more simple way of seeing how things in nature are relational is to consider how they have common origins. According to Bonaventure, this is how Francis saw things. About Francis, Bonaventure writes:

> *The consideration of the common origin of all creatures filled him with overflowing tenderness for all; and he called them all his brothers and sisters, because they had all one origin with himself.* (1261, 78)

Here Bonaventure points out that Francis saw himself existing in relationship with all creatures, and called each one of them "brother" and "sister." And this is for the simple fact that all creatures have the same father, namely, God. Further, in Francis' poem "The Canticle of the Creatures" (1225), he not only talks of "sister bodily death" but also "brother sun," "sister moon," "brother wind," "sister water," "brother fire," and "sister Mother Earth" (see appendix 3). Francis also read the Bible, and had favorite passages from it. We can thus see how Francis participates in the Catholic tradition, since, as we first saw in Paul's letters, the Catholic tradition holds that we can know about God through the Bible, through reason, and through creation.

We have mentioned how Francis' approach to ethics has much in common with a Christian virtue ethics that is firmly grounded in the New Testament. In his poem "The Canticle of the Creatures," we can also see how the Old Testament of the Bible was influential in his views. The book of Genesis from the Old Testament, for example, describes how God is responsible for all of creation and God saw it all as good.

> God called the dry land "the earth," and the basin of the water he called "the sea." God saw how good it was. Then God said, "Let the earth bring forth vegetation: every kind of plant that bears seed and every kind of fruit tree on earth that bears fruit with its seed in it."

*And so it happened: the earth brought forth every kind of plant that
bears seed and every kind of fruit tree with its seed in it. God saw
how good it was. ... Then God said, "Let the water teem with an
abundance of living creatures, and on the earth let birds fly beneath
the dome of the sky." And so it happened ... God saw how good
it was. ... Then God said, "Let the earth bring forth all kinds of living creatures" ... And so it happened ... God saw how good it was.
(Genesis 1:10–25)*

This theme is continued in the book of Psalms in the Old Testament:

*Praise the Lord from the heavens, praise him in the heights ... Praise
him sun and moon; praise him, all you shining stars. Praise him, you
highest heavens ... Let them praise the name of the Lord, for he commanded and they were created; He established them forever and ever;
he gave them a duty which shall not pass away. Praise the Lord from
the earth, you sea monsters and all depths; Fire and hail, snow and
mist, storm winds that fulfill his word; You mountains and all you
hills, you fruit trees and all you cedars; You wild beasts and all tame
animals, you creeping things and you winged fowl. (Psalms 148:1–10)*

And the theme is continued in the book of Daniel from the Old Testament:

*Blessed are you, O Lord, the God of our fathers, praiseworthy and
exalted above all forever; And blessed in your holy and glorious name,
praiseworthy and exalted above all for all ages ... Bless the Lord, all
you works of the Lord, praise and exalt him above all forever ... You
heavens, bless the Lord, praise and exalt him above all forever ... Sun
and moon, bless the Lord; praise and exalt him above all forever, Stars of
heaven, bless the Lord; praise and exalt him above all forever ... All you
winds, bless the Lord; praise and exalt him above all forever, Fire and
heat, bless the Lord; praise and exalt him above all forever ... Nights
and days, bless the Lord ... Let the earth bless the Lord ... Mountains
and hills, bless the Lord ... Everything growing from the earth, bless the
Lord ... Seas and rivers, bless the Lord ... All you birds of the air ...
All you beasts, wild and tame, bless the Lord. (Daniel 3:52–81)*

Like the author of Daniel, and the author of the book of Psalms, Francis, in
his poem, praises God for the goodness in creation.

For the Franciscan tradition, understanding God as creator and as responsible for the goodness of creation is a crucial insight of utmost importance. Bonaventure, as a Franciscan philosopher, shares this conviction. He often uses the image of a *book* to describe God and creation. Bonaventure writes:

> *the universe is like a book reflecting, representing, and describing its Maker, the Trinity.* (1257: 104)

5.4 Human Dignity and Dignity of Creation: Scotus

The philosopher John Duns Scotus (1265–1308) is another famous Franciscan. He is well known for his highly technical and intricate style of philosophical analysis. In 1966 Pope Paul VI published a short work called *Alma Parens* in which he states that Scotus' work is a "valuable theological treasure" and that "Saint Francis of Assisi's most beautiful ideal of perfection" is "embedded in the work of Scotus and inflame it" (Pope Paul VI 1966, 106, 105).

Other Popes, too, have noted the value and importance of Scotus' works. According to the authors of a book about Scotus:

> *No fewer than twelve supreme pontiffs of the Roman Catholic Church, from Alexander VI in 1501 to John Paul II in 1980, have endorsed the teachings of Scotus as one of the glories of the Franciscan Order.* (Wolter and O'Neill 1993, 1)

In fact, in 1993 Pope John Paul II honored Scotus with the title of "blessed," so today he is known as "Blessed John Duns Scotus." Recently, Pope Benedict XVI wrote about "the important contribution that Duns Scotus made to the history of theology" (Pope Benedict XVI 2011, 136–137).

As a Catholic theologian, Scotus upholds that human beings can know about God through the use of reason (Duns Scotus 1300 I, 14–33). In his youth, Scotus became "attracted to the Franciscan way of life" (Wolter and O'Neill 1993, 13). In Scotus' ethical writings, he argues that human beings have free choice (1302a IV, 151–152). He upholds that the natural law is written on the human heart; and that human beings can know the difference between right and wrong (1302a II, 162–66; 1302a IV, 195–198). He discusses the moral goodness of human actions (1302a I, 167–168). He explains how the Ten Commandments relate to natural law (1302a III, 198–207).

He discusses human law and divine law (1302b IV, 29–47). He also writes about happiness (1302a IV, 155–162), the virtues (1302a III, 223–292), the principle of charity (1302a III, 275–292), justice (1302a IV, 183–191), and property rights (1302b IV, 29–47).

A novel and important contribution that Scotus makes to ethical theory is his way of describing what it means to be an individual. In prior chapters we have seen how the Catholic tradition regards each individual as significant, since each individual is made in the image and likeness of God. Francis, too, respected each individual that God created; each one is a brother or a sister.

Scotus continues with this and makes the further philosophical case that since God creates freely, each person is *unique* in all time and for all eternity (Nothwehr 2005, 48). Scotus engages with the philosophical question of what makes one thing different from another, what makes it an individual? Scotus makes the case that each individual is a unique particular, a "this." In Latin, the word *this* is *haec.* So the special individuality that "makes a singular thing what it is and differentiates it from all other things" can be called *haecceitas*, which literally means "thisness" (Nothwehr 2005, 48).

Another way to look at it is to say that a "human person's identity cannot be reduced to his or her physical make-up or current embodied existence" (Nothwehr 2005, 48). There is more to an individual than a physical body, and even more than a spiritual soul. Individuals, because they are unique, are "incapable of duplication" (Wolter and O'Neill 1993, 28).

In chapter 3 we noted that in the modern period of Catholic ethics the concept of individual moral rights gets used more and more. Scotus' concept of haecceitas helps us to see the dignity and worth that individuals possess and their moral rights that deserve to be respected. Because an individual has *dignity* and *rights*, we, in turn, have *duties* to respect that dignity and those rights.

Scotus' concept of haecceitas points us toward "the dignity of each individual (both persons and objects) as a unique and irreplaceable contribution to the whole of reality" (Ingham and Shannon 1993, 63). Notice that Scotus' concept of haecceitas applies not only to persons, but to all of creation (Nothwehr 2005, 48). Scotus sees a natural goodness of creation (Duns Scotus 1302a II, 176). God chose each thing, not a different thing; this invests value in each individual. Scotus' concept of haecceitas thus flows from Francis' regarding each element in creation as brother and sister.

As Francis and Bonaventure did, Scotus saw the natural world as relational. Human beings are part of the relational natural world. Ethically, human beings can naturally flourish as relational creatures. As one scholar on Scotus puts it, Scotus develops the view that "human development requires relational living" (Ingham 2012, 222).

The idea of relational living ties in with how Catholic social teaching endorses both the personalist principle and the principle of the common good at the same time. Because one recognizes the dignity of the individual, that does not mean one can disregard the common good. And because one recognizes the importance and value of common good, that does not mean one can disregard the individual. With his concept of haecceitas regarding individuals and his view of a relational creation derived from a relational creator, Scotus helps to shed light on the relationship of the individual and the community.

5.5 Franciscan Care Ethics

Several aspects of Franciscan ethics have come to be seen as particularly significant in the light of recent developments in ethical theory. Some ethical theorists in the twentieth century have noted that an ethics firmly rooted in care is much different from an ethics solely rooted in a commitment to ethical principles. As we saw in chapter 3 on modern Catholic ethics, for example, an emphasis on duties and obligations as the central overriding ethical principle can overshadow other important dimensions of ethics. One who acts solely out of principle may seem impersonal, for instance, and thus the personal dimension of ethics becomes overshadowed.

Francis of Assisi advocated for an ethic that was personal, not impersonal (Chesterton 1923, 40). Francis did not view ethical actions as simply required by principle, duty, or obligation (Dennis et al. 1993, 154). Francis held that acting out of care and concern is more important and more genuine than acting out of principle. Francis writes:

> Let each one confidently make known his need to another that the other
> might discover what is needed and minister to him. Let each one love
> and care for his brother as a mother loves and cares for her son in those
> matters in which God has given him the grace. (1221, chp 9)

In the twentieth century, an ethic that recommends attending to the needs of concrete particular persons with genuine care and compassion came to be known as *care ethics*, or an ethics of care.

A few more points will help us to see that Francis supported a care ethics. For instance, care ethics emphasizes that human beings are *relational beings*. Yet this fundamental fact about human beings, care ethicists claim, can be forgotten and overlooked. Some highly individualistic people will even try to deny it! Care ethics asks us to notice the many relationships we are in with other persons. Here, we are not talking about abstract relationships, but actual personal relationships with particular people. Being attentive to the many personal relationships we are in can shed light on what it is we should do; that is, this attentiveness can shed light on what is ethical. Committing ourselves to an abstract ethical principle can blind us from seeing the needs of those who are closest to us. Francis, too, viewed humans as *relational beings*, and he held that a caring person is motivated to act ethically not out of duty or commitment, but out of caring and love (Delio 2003, 14).

As noted, care ethics asks us to notice the many relationships we are in with other persons. Francis held that God is one of those persons. For Francis, we are in relation with God, whether we acknowledge it or not. As we discussed in the context of Bonaventure, since God is three persons in one, God is a relational being. The very essence of God has a relational dimension. Further, though, Christianity teaches that human beings can enter into personal relationship with God. Francis himself had a loving relationship with Jesus (Delio 2003, 11).

Now, what would be the ideal relationship between a human person and God? It would be a loving relationship, which brings feelings of joy. As Augustine said, happiness is the joy that comes through loving God. Franciscan care ethics says that to be ethical we must attend to those with whom we are in relationship, God included.

Another aspect of us as relational beings is that we are in relationship with nature. Creation—the natural world—is relational, too. As demonstrated by Francis, each individual of the natural world is to be regarded as a brother or sister, which highlights the personal relationship between humans and the natural world. Francis saw "God's goodness in every aspect of creation" (Delio 2003, 16). As with his stance toward fellow human beings, "Francis' respect for creation was not a duty or obligation but arose out of an inner love" (Delio 2003, 14).

One last aspect of Franciscan care ethics to notice is how it relates to Franciscan virtue ethics, as discussed in section 5.2. Is Franciscan care ethics different and distinct from Franciscan virtue ethics? This same question was asked of care ethics when it was first identified as a distinct ethic in the twentieth century. It seems most sensible to regard care ethics as a particular kind of virtue ethics. For, after all, we could view *care* itself as a virtue. We could view care as a trait or characteristic of persons. We could ask, for example, are you a caring person? Are you an uncaring person?

The Christian tradition holds that charity is the most important virtue. How can we concretely put charity into action? By caring. Caring and service for others is an essential dimension of Franciscan ethics, and a key ethical ideal. Since we ourselves are made in God's image and likeness and have dignity, caring for ourselves is also not to be neglected. In the next chapter we will consider specific examples of caring for self and caring for others.

5.6 Conclusion

In this chapter we have considered some events in the life of St. Francis of Assisi, and we have observed his commitment to Catholic ethics. In his nativity scene at Christmas in the year 1223, for instance, Francis illustrated how God is present, relational, and overflowing love. Francis' beliefs about God set the foundation for his ethical approach. His commitment to Christian ethics, as spelled out in the Gospels, includes a commitment to Christian ethical principles such as the principle of charity, the Golden Rule, the personalist principle, and the principle of the preferential option for the poor, as well as a commitment to Christian virtues. Jesus was Francis' role model. Francis believed that Christians should be humble, compassionate, peaceful, kind, gentle, and forgiving. In addition, Francis upheld the Catholic ethical view that true joy and happiness are found in relationship with Jesus.

This chapter also looked at how during the medieval period of history the Franciscan philosophers Bonaventure and Scotus sought to further Francis' ethical insights and thereby contribute to the development of the Catholic ethical tradition. God is relational love, Bonaventure clarified, and human beings are called to enter into loving personal relationship with God. Creation, as a reflection of God's goodness, is also relational, so human beings are likewise called to enter into loving personal relationship with the individuals in creation, which are our brothers and sisters.

Each individual is loved by God and each is in a unique relationship with God. Scotus' concept of haecceitas is a reflection of Francis' insight that all creatures of God's creation enjoy the status of brother and sister, since they all share the same father; haecceitas is also a reflection of the Biblical pronouncement that God calls each one by name (Isaiah 43:1; John 10:3; CCC sec 2158; *Compendium* 2005, sec 61). Each individual creature has unique value because it has a unique place in creation and a unique relationship with God. With its commitment to feelings of joy and love, concrete personal relationships, and call for caring and compassionate service to others, Franciscan ethics finds a natural home among care ethics.

Franciscan ethics occupies a central place in the Catholic ethical tradition. In 1882 on the 700th anniversary of the birth of St. Francis, Pope Leo XIII published a document called *On St. Francis of Assisi*. In that document Pope Leo described St. Francis as a model Christian that everyone should imitate. Leo said that St. Francis was helpful to the people living in the twelfth century, and just as helpful as a model in 1882.

When Pope John Paul II invited the world's religious leaders to meet together and pray for peace, he chose Assisi for the meeting place. Why? It is because Pope John Paul II regarded Assisi as "the city of St. Francis" (1987, para 47). In a public speech, during Pope John Paul II's first visit to Assisi as pope, he prayed to Saint Francis of Assisi:

> You, who brought Christ so close to your age, help us to bring Christ
> close to our age, to our difficult and critical times. Help us! (1978, 8)

When trying to demonstrate to the world's religious leaders that the Catholic Church is committed to peace, John Paul II invited them to Assisi, four times (1986, 1993, 1999, and 2002).

Also, today, when someone asks for the Catholic view on creation and care of creation, what name repeatedly comes up? Francis of Assisi. In 1979, Pope John Paul II named Francis of Assisi the patron saint of ecology. The pope wrote:

> Among the holy and admirable men who have revered nature as a
> wonderful gift of God to the human race, St Francis of Assisi deserves
> special consideration. For he, in a special way, deeply sensed the
> universal works of the Creator and, filled with a certain divine spirit,

sang that very beautiful "Canticle of the Creatures." Through them,
Brother Sun most powerful and Sister Moon and the stars of heaven,
he offered fitting praise, glory, honour and all blessing to the most high,
all-powerful, good Lord … Therefore, we proclaim St Francis of Assisi
heavenly Patron of those who promote ecology. (1979)

In a speech in 2007 for the Celebration of the World Day of Peace, Pope Benedict XVI said: "The poem-prayer of Saint Francis, known as 'the Canticle of Brother Sun,' is a wonderful and ever timely example of [a] multifaceted ecology of peace." Even more recently, Pope Benedict XVI, in his book *The Virtues* (2010), wrote about Francis as well.

In the light of the Gospel Beatitudes we can understand the gentleness
with which St. Francis was able to live his relations with others, present-
ing himself in humility to all and becoming a witness and artisan of
peace. (2010, 31)

And in his book *Great Teachers* (2011), Pope Benedict XVI wrote:

Francis was a great saint and a joyful man. His simplicity, his humil-
ity, his faith, his love for Christ, his goodness toward every man and
every woman, brought him gladness in every circumstance. (2011, 76)

In 2013, when Pope Benedict XVI stepped down, a new pope was elected, and he chose the name Francis, in honor of St. Francis of Assisi. Today Pope Francis brings the message of St. Francis to people around the world.

Having spelled out the various dimensions of Catholic ethics, and how Franciscan ethics fits into the Catholic tradition, the next chapter will apply Catholic Franciscan ethics to particular ethical issues—both personal ethical issues and social ethical issues. These issues include: respect and care for self, care for human life, care for the marginalized, and care for the Earth.

Concepts, Principles, Theories, and Traditions Introduced in Chapter 5

Concepts

Manger

Incarnation

Humility of the incarnation

Joy

Haecceitas

God as relational

Creation as relational

Human beings as relational

Relational love

Theories

Care ethics

Traditions

Franciscan

Review Questions

1. In 1223, what did Francis do in the town of Greccio? Why?
2. What does the phrase *humility of the incarnation* mean?
3. What did Francis' biographer Thomas of Celano say about Francis that fits into a virtue ethics model?
4. Of the following kinds of law, which kind was the most explicitly influential in Francis' ethical approach? Eternal law, divine law (old law, new law), natural law, or human law?
5. In addition to the seven traditional Christian virtues, which other virtues did Francis emphasize?
6. Of the following ethical theories (virtue ethics, deontological ethics, or care ethics), which one seems to fit the *least* with Francis' ethical approach? Explain.

Discussion Questions

1. Review the circumstances in which Francis came upon a person with leprosy. Explain what happened in terms of virtue ethics and care ethics.

2. Review the circumstances in which Francis met with the Islamic leader Sultan Malek al-Kamil. Explain what happened in terms of virtue ethics and care ethics.

3. Is there really any difference between Franciscan virtue ethics and Franciscan care ethics? Explain.

4. Review the principles of Catholic social teaching that are listed in diagram 4.5. Which of them are most apparent in Franciscan ethics? Explain.

5. Review what Augustine and Aquinas said about just war theory, and then try to formulate a Franciscan approach to just war theory.

6. Read Francis' poem "The Canticle of the Creatures" (1225) in appendix 3 of this book. List all of the moral virtues you find in it. What is the ethical significance of the last word of the poem?

6

CATHOLIC FRANCISCAN ETHICS: SOME APPLICATIONS

In the little town of Gubbio, located about thirty-three miles north of Assisi, the townspeople lived in fear of a large, fierce wolf. Francis felt compassion for these people who were living in fear, so he put his trust in God and went to find the wolf. Francis found the wolf and spoke to him: "I desire, Brother Wolf, to make peace between you and them, so that you may offend no more, and they shall forgive you and all your past offences, and neither man nor dogs shall pursue you any more." And Francis offered to the wolf that the people would provide food to the wolf, since Francis believed that hunger was probably the cause of the wolf's actions against the people of Gubbio. For the next two years, the wolf seemed to agree to the peace agreement, until the wolf died of old age.

This is one of the many stories about Francis that are gathered in a small book called *The Little Flowers of St. Francis of Assisi* (Alger 1390, chp 21), written anonymously about one hundred years after Francis' death. Scholars tell us that we should not take the story of the wolf literally, but that it still accurately conveys Francis' ethical approach. One ethical aspect of the story is how Francis views creation; in the story he respects the wolf as a member of God's creation, calling the wolf his "brother." Another ethical aspect is that Francis seeks peace between warring parties through communication and compromise; in the story he works out an agreement between the wolf and the townspeople by getting to the root of the dispute, which Francis identifies as the wolf's hunger. Francis' 1219 pilgrimage for peace to the Middle East is another example of how Francis attempted to live up to Jesus' directive for Christians to be peacemakers (Alger 1390, chp 24).

6.1 Respect and Care for Self: Personal Ethical Issues

Each individual faces multiple ethical issues. To clarify the different kinds of ethical issues we can encounter, it is helpful to distinguish between ethical issues that center on (a) caring for self and those that center on (b) caring for others. With regard to caring for others we can further distinguish between (b1) caring for other human beings, (b2) for other human beings who are marginalized, and (b3) caring for creation, the Earth.

First, what would a Catholic Franciscan ethics say about (a) caring for oneself? Let's sketch out an answer to that question by drawing from Francis, Bonaventure, and Scotus. From Francis we can see that respect and care for self involves working to develop virtues in oneself, virtues such as mercy, compassion, humility, self-discipline, courage, temperance, simplicity, self-restraint, and patience (Bonaventure 1261, chp 5). Humbly caring for oneself is different from being preoccupied with oneself, and also different from acting selfishly. Francis knew the dangers of being overly concerned with oneself, and he knew that a Christian ethic encourages us to strive for humility, not for honors. In the following quotation Bonaventure explains how Francis requested that his friars (his brothers) be called friars *minor* to help them remind themselves to be humble.

> From humility ... Francis desired that his friars should be called minors ... to fulfil the words of the Gospel ... and also that his disciples might learn by the very name they bear that they have come to the school of the ... Master of humility, Jesus Christ. (1261, chp 6)

For Francis, another very important aspect of caring for oneself includes taking time for prayer, reflection, and contemplation. Many times in his life Francis took the time to be alone with God in order to discern what direction to steer his life. In the introduction to *CFE* we saw an example of a prayer that Francis created, "The Prayer before the Crucifix." His poem "The Canticle of the Creatures" is really a prayer, too. Francis considered prayer to be vital nourishment for himself, and we can tell from his writings that he enjoyed composing prayers (1221, chps 17, 21). His first biographer said that Francis would engage in self-examination daily (Celano 1229, Book I, chp 16).

Francis' role model was Jesus, and the Bible describes many occasions upon which Jesus would take time to pray. At different times in his life, Francis would go by himself to the woods or a cave in order to pray (Noonan and Gasnick 1987, 8, 32). Francis set aside time to be alone, to encounter nature, to pray to God, to give God thanks, and to seek guidance (Bonaventure 1261, chp 1).

But praying is not only about withdrawing from the world. While it is true that through prayer and refection we can look inward to our inner depths, we can also look outward and become conscious of God's presence in the world. The nativity scene that Francis organized at Greccio is an example of how Francis tried to get people to look at the world reflectively and experience God's presence in the world. The same is true with regard to his attitude toward creation. The natural world is God's creation, so reflecting on creation can help us in our relationship with God. Being mindful of the presence of God at all moments has ethical dimensions, and for Francis, "the awareness of God's presence shaped how he lived every moment" (Dennis et al. 1993, 147).

For Francis, the activity of prayerful reflection is accompanied with feelings of pleasure and joy. From developing a deeper relationship with God, and a closeness to God, we can experience joy. And for Francis, the same is true about our relationship with creation. Since creation is a reflection of God, a closeness to creation can also yield joy.

Bonaventure describes how Francis, who is commonly thought of as a model of Christian moral virtue, should also be considered a model of contemplation and reflection (1259, chp 7). Francis had a spiritual experience while he was in contemplation on Mount Alverno. Bonaventure visited this place and was inspired to write the *Journey of the Mind to God* (1259, 38). In that work we can see that for Bonaventure also, respect and care for self involves self-reflection. Bonaventure argued that human beings can strive for increasing levels of knowledge, which can ultimately lead to the love of God (1259, 103). In *Journey of the Mind to God* (1259) Bonaventure describes the human mind's climb to successive levels of reality through six progressive stages of illumination, until God is finally understood as *the good*. Bonaventure believes that when we introspect and enter within ourselves, we can move ever more closely to God's divine light that radiates within us. For Bonaventure, this inner divine light can illuminate the truth of our lives and the truth of the world around us.

A virtue ethics is part of this process that Bonaventure describes, since to transport oneself through the stages of illumination one must achieve self-mastery. This kind of spiritual progress and development can only realistically occur through determination and self-discipline. A Franciscan virtue ethics model encourages the development of good habits that can lead to a deeper and deeper relationship with God. Not only can good habits lead to deeper self-reflection, but the process could work in the opposite direction, in that self-reflection can lead to deepening of virtues. Bonaventure makes this point when he says "true self-knowledge" can lead to "true humility" (1260, chps 1 and 2). Put simply, self-examination is a path toward humility (see diagram 6.1).

Diagram 6.1

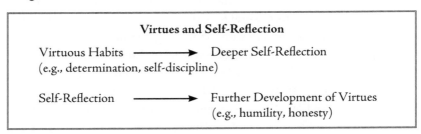

Virtues and Self-Reflection

Virtuous Habits ⟶ Deeper Self-Reflection
(e.g., determination, self-discipline)

Self-Reflection ⟶ Further Development of Virtues
(e.g., humility, honesty)

For Bonaventure, another aspect of caring for oneself for spiritual achievement is avoiding sin. Bonaventure argues that sin darkens the mind and enslaves one to experiences of the five senses. So sin distracts us from fully entering within and moving toward our inner divine light (1259, 103–104). Bonaventure believes that ethical behavior that is in keeping with the scriptures and the theological virtues helps to cleanse ourselves, so that we can have more openness to achieving deeper levels of understanding.

Scotus, too, views self-mastery and self-determination as key for moral growth. As one Scotus scholar sums it up:

> The heart of Scotus's moral paradigm is self-determination ... And yet, self-determination is not the moral goal, but only the first step to realizing what it means to be rational, relational, and to live a life of creative meaning and value. (Ingham 2012, 63)

In a similar manner, the following passage written by Franciscan scholar Dawn Nothwehr, sums up Scotus' virtue ethic. (Bear in mind that a synonym for virtue is *perfection*). "In Scotus' ethical thought," Nothwehr writes,

> *the focus is on the person; the object of moral science is the perfection of the moral person. (2005, 56)*

Scotus' concept of haecceitas, as we've seen, points to the dignity of each individual. Care and respect for self requires respect for one's *own* dignity.

Catholic ethics sometimes distinguishes between *life ethics* and *social ethics* (Pope Benedict XVI 2009, para 15). Benedict mentions the two documents, *Humanae Vitae* (1968) by Pope Paul VI and *Evangelium Vitae* (1995) by John Paul II, as both focusing on *life ethics*—the individual life that each of us possesses. Life ethics includes all human life, including one's own; so life ethics includes care and respect for oneself. The individual human person has dignity (is a *thisness*). Thus, the view that each of us is a human person made in the image and likeness of God calls us to care for self. Pope Benedict XVI says the Church forcefully maintains a link between *life ethics* and *social ethics* (2009, para 15). Examples of social ethics appear in the many documents on Catholic social teaching that we have looked at in a previous chapter, documents that point to our ethical responsibilities regarding other people in our society.

Let us now return to Catholic social ethics, and see what *Catholic Franciscan social ethics* looks like.

6.2 Respect and Care for Human Life: Social Justice

For Francis, respect and care for human life involves several dimensions. Ethically, we should recognize all human beings as brothers and sisters who are made in the image of likeness of God who have dignity. The contemporary Catholic principle known as the *personalist principle*, which says that the human person is made in the image of God and has dignity that ought to be respected, is consistent with Francis' insight that we are all brothers and sisters. In addition, the contemporary Catholic principle known as the *principle of solidarity*, which says that we must be determined to commit ourselves in solidarity to the good of all, also fits here very well. The term *solidarity* signifies a sense of unity between people: we are all part of one family.

The appropriate attitude toward our brothers and sisters is to love and care for them and help them achieve happiness. Bonaventure supports this and says that respect and care for human life involves charity to others (1257, 212–213). Bonaventure endorses the twofold commandment of love and upholds that we should have respect for our neighbor (1257, 215–216).

Scotus also reminds us that respect and care for human life involves attending to one's loving relationships: one's family and society (Ingham 2003, 123–124). We might call this "relational living" (Ingham 2012, 222). For Scotus, the way toward unity with others is through a relationship of love (Delio et al. 2008, 92). Think again how this fits with what the Church calls *solidarity*.

Caring for one's brothers and sisters comes with its own set of special challenges. These challenges can become even greater when we encounter brothers and sisters who seem very different from us. Yet Catholic Franciscan ethics calls us to respect and care for those who are similar *and* those who are different from us. The issue of difference is known as *diversity*.

For Francis, given the diversity of God's creation, we should expect diversity among the human community and respect those who appear different from us (Blow 2003, unit 8). In Francis' day, Church leaders were predominantly men, but Francis' commitment to viewing each individual as a brother and sister led him to include women in his community of followers. St. Clare of Assisi, for example, was one of Francis' early followers (Dennis et al. 1993, 50).

A typical Franciscan way to care and respect someone who is very different is by invitation. Franciscans gently invite others to share their outlook and their lifestyle. They simply offer to share what has brought meaning to their individual lives. We might call this a dialogue approach. This dialogue approach appears in the Vatican II document *Nostra Aetate* (the English translation of the title is "Our Time"). *Nostra Aetate* recommends that Catholics should dialogue with followers of other religions (*Documents of Vatican II*, 1966). A Catholic and Franciscan ethics does not force beliefs on others. Beliefs, values, and principles are simply offered—shared—and others are free to embrace them or reject them.

Franciscans, then, endorse a nonviolent way of interacting with others, because they see this as fitting for Christians. Recall Jesus' Beatitudes from chapter 1 (section 1.2): the path to blessedness and happiness, said Jesus, is through forgiveness and peacemaking, not through aggression and hostility. A nonviolent approach is a specific way to respect others. This is especially true with regard to one's enemies. Think of the story of the wolf of Gubbio.

A natural response of the townspeople would be to see the wolf as an enemy that must be eliminated with violent force. Yet, as we saw at the beginning of this chapter, Francis took a nonviolent approach to the situation, not a violent one. In his nonviolent approach to peacemaking, we see again how Francis takes Jesus as his role model. It was Jesus who first said to love one's enemies. The Catholic tradition regards Jesus as the prince of peace. Jesus said that those who live by the sword (violently) will die by the sword (Matthew 26:52). Francis took this teaching of Jesus seriously and literally and recommended it to his friars. According to Bonaventure, the peace that "Jesus Christ proclaimed" was the "message of peace" that

> Francis announced over and over, proclaiming it at the beginning and the end of his sermons. Every greeting of his became a wish for peace. (1259, 35)

To this day, Franciscans continue to follow Francis' example and often greet people with the expression *pace e bene*, which translated from Italian to English means "peace and good." Francis was firmly committed to living out Jesus' call for us to become peacemakers, and Francis is well known for this. Recall that, as mentioned at the end of the last chapter, Pope John Paul II invited the world's religious leaders to Francis' town of Assisi four times to pray for peace.

6.3 Respect and Care for the Marginalized: Social Justice

For Francis, respect and care for the marginalized include concern for helping and healing the sick: lepers for instance, as we saw in the previous chapter (sections 5.1 and 5.2). As noted, Francis believed that we should recognize all human beings as brothers and sisters, and this included lepers and the sick, too. One story is told in *The Little Flowers of St. Francis of Assisi* of how Francis approached a leper and said, "God grant thee peace, my beloved brother" (Alger 1390, chp 25). Further, think of the symbolic significance of the first time Francis found it in himself to hug and kiss a leper he encountered (Bonaventure 1261, chp 1). To hug and kiss someone is a sign of a willingness to enter into a close loving relationship with that person.

Although in Francis' day lepers were marginalized by society and treated as outcasts required to live outside the walls of the town, Francis still saw them as brothers and sisters deserving of respect and care. Francis, in following the example of Jesus who had shown compassion to lepers, believed it was the will of God to show compassion to lepers. As noted in section 5.1, both Jesus and Francis upheld what the Catholic tradition today calls the *personalist principle*: as human beings, lepers are made in the image and likeness of God, and therefore deserve our care and respect. Also noted in section 5.1 was that Jesus and Francis upheld what the Catholic tradition today calls the *principle of the preferential option for the poor*: the poor are made in the image and likeness of God, just as much as any human person. And yet the poor—those who are vulnerable, and those who are poor in health—are in most need; therefore, the needs of the poor, including lepers, should have an urgent claim on our conscience.

Lepers were not the only people marginalized in Francis' time, though. Joseph Chinnici, a Franciscan scholar, has described how Francis' culture— medieval Italy—had

> developed *rituals of exclusion to protect itself both economically and culturally from the threatening presence of the other, symbolically identified as "leper" or "heretic" or "criminal" or "infidel."* (2003, xi)

Bonaventure, in keeping with Francis' approach, upholds that respect and care for the marginalized includes viewing marginalized groups—whether lepers or criminals, for example—as related and connected to us. Again, they are connected to us as brothers and sisters, and so we should extend to them the same relational love as we would to anyone.

Scotus' concept of haecceitas also applies to members of marginalized groups. Each person still has unique dignity, even if he or she has been marginalized by society. Also, Scotus' notion that human development requires relational living supports an inclusive attitude toward those members of society who are in need of aid and who find themselves detached from loving relationships. The very idea of "marginalized" means "put on the margins" and "not important." Such an attitude toward human persons does not acknowledge their *haecceity*, their dignity and true value.

In section 6.2 we saw how the personalist principle and the principle of solidarity are involved in respecting and caring for others, and in this section above we considered the principle of the preferential option for the poor. In addition, two more principles from Catholic social teaching that have to do with concern for the marginalized are the *principle of the common good* and the *principle of the universal destination of goods*.

According to the Catholic principle known as the *principle of the universal destination of goods*, God destined the earth and all it contains for all peoples (*Compendium of Catholic Social Teaching* 2005, secs 171–184; see diagram 4.5 in chapter 4). In order to achieve a state of well-being, people need to use and have access to the materials and fruits of the earth. God, as the creator, meant these goods to be used by all. As the *Compendium* states:

> God gave the earth to the whole human race for the sustenance of all its members, without excluding or favoring anyone. (sec 171)

How this principle specifically relates to respect and care for the marginalized is explained in the following quotation from the *Compendium*:

> The principle of the universal destination of goods *requires that the poor, the marginalized and in all cases those whose living conditions interfere with their proper growth should be the focus of particular concern. (sec 182)

The *principle of the common good* is another closely related principle. This principle states that there is a common good that humanity is responsible for ensuring and attaining (secs 160–184; see diagram 4.5 in chapter 4). According to this principle, the "common good ... involves all members of society" (sec 167). It is our ethical responsibility to promote the common good, which includes all members of society, including those who may be marginalized.

These ethical principles prompt us, then, to ask ourselves: who are marginalized in our society *today*? The authors of a book about St. Francis offer the following suggestion for thinking about marginalized persons today.

> We know that today the leper is not only a single individual whom we might encounter as we go out from familiar to new realities. Today the leper is the thousands of homeless ... the numberless battered women ... the deinstitutionalized mental patient ... the "third world" hungry ... the children of impoverished countries. (Dennis et al. 1993, 25)

And,

> In the world today, the lives of marginalized people in El Salvador, Guatemala, the Middle East, Bolivia, Peru, the Philippines, Korea, South Africa, and the cities and rural areas of our own country as well, are inextricably linked to our own. (Dennis et al. 1993, 22–23)

These authors suggest that a Franciscan ethical response to this situation is that

> We are invited to move step by step ... into greater solidarity with the poor and with Christ who is incarnate on the margins of society. (Dennis et al. 1993, 23)

In addition to recognizing all human beings as brothers and sisters, we saw in chapter 5 how Francis in fact recognized *all* God's creatures—human and nonhuman, living and nonliving—as brothers and sisters (see "Canticle," appendix 3).

6.4 Respect and Care for the Earth: Environmental Justice

For Francis, we should also extend respect and care *beyond* the human community. We see how Francis himself tried to live in such a way through many examples of how he interacted with swallows, turtledoves, rabbits, fish, lambs, sheep, wolves, worms, bees, and flowers—all of which he regarded as creatures of God's creation, and therefore his brothers and sisters (Celano 1229, Book I, chp 29). Francis also showed great love for the farmlands around Assisi and for the mountains, rivers, and forests (Dennis et al. 1993, 104).

In his "Canticle," Francis writes:

> Praise be You, my Lord, with all Your creatures especially Sir Brother Sun ... Praised be You, my Lord, through Sister Moon and the stars ... Praised be You, my Lord, through Brother wind ... Praised by You, my Lord, through Sister Water ... Praised be You, my Lord, through Brother Fire ... Praised be You, my Lord, through our Sister Mother Earth, who sustains us and governs us, and who produces various fruit with colored flowers and herbs. (1225; see appendix 3)

As we saw in section 5.3, Francis viewed the world around him as the creation of a good God. *Everything* in creation, then, has a value ultimately derivable from God. In ethical terms, it has been said that "Francis' respect for creation was not a duty or obligation but arose out of an inner love" (Delio 2003, 14).

Bonaventure, too, sought to explain the important relationship between the Creator and creation (1257, part II, chps 1–12). Creation is a book of nature, Bonaventure says; the created world is

> like a book reflecting, representing, and describing its Maker, the Trinity. (1257, part II, chp 12, 104)

Bonaventure sees creation as relational, like the Trinity of Love, and a loving outflow (Delio 2003, 22–23).

Scotus sees a natural goodness in creation (Duns Scotus 1302a II, 176). Further though, according to Scotus, God taking on human flesh in the form of Jesus actually contributes to the fulfillment of creation. As mentioned in section 5.1, the idea that God has taken on human flesh in the form of Jesus is known as the *incarnation*. In Scotus' way of thinking, then, creation itself is the beginning of the incarnation, since for Jesus to be born of flesh and blood implies that these materials would first have to exist before the incarnation can happen (Osborne 2003, 60). Pope Benedict XVI summarizes that

> in the opinion of Duns Scotus, the Incarnation of the Son of God, planned for all eternity by God the Father at the level of love is the fulfillment of creation and enables every creature, in Christ and through Christ, to be filled with grace and to praise and glorify God in eternity. (2011, 137)

This is an important teaching of Scotus, because Scotus uses it to justify his innovative position that "the Son of God would have been made man even if humanity had not sinned" (Pope Benedict XVI 2011, 137). As one Franciscan scholar has described Scotus' point: "The incarnation is not a divine after-thought, occasioned by human sin. Rather, the incarnation has a firstness that coincides with the firstness of creation" (Osborne 2003, 60). Again, Pope Benedict XVI has recently summarized how Scotus connects the ideas of incarnation with creation:

> Incarnation … is God's original idea of ultimately uniting with himself the whole of creation, in the Person and Flesh of the Son." (2011, 137)

The upshot here is that creation—the natural environment—the Earth—is not merely the backdrop for human lives. The Franciscan tradition sees the Earth as playing an intimate role in God's plan for humanity.

But there is more. In section 5.4 we saw that Scotus' concept of haecceitas applies not only to persons, but to all of creation (Nothwehr 2005, 48). The Franciscan scholar Mary Beth Ingham has noted that: "A striking feature of Scotist texts is the importance the Franciscan places upon the individuality of each creature" (Ingham 2012, 33). God chose each thing, not a different thing; and so this invests value in each individual. Scotus' concept of haecceitas logically flows from the way Francis regarded each element in creation as brother and sister.

Further, and also from section 5.4, we saw that Scotus, as Francis and Bonaventure did, saw the natural world as relational. Human beings are part of the relational natural world. Ethically, then, human beings can only naturally flourish as relational creatures. As Ingham puts it, Scotus develops the view that "human development requires relational living" (2012, 222). Scotus, therefore, recommends a loving relationship with creation—not an abstract loving relationship that pays lips service to theoretical ideals—but a loving relationship in which concrete individuals engage in caring and respectful acts toward the Earth (Delio 2003, 37).

A Catholic and Franciscan perspective on the natural environment has also found its way into the recent *Catechism of the Catholic Church*. The *Catechism* addresses the topic of respect for the integrity of creation, and there it says that "we should recall the gentleness with which saints like St. Francis of Assisi ... treated animals" (1992, sec 2416). Recall also from section 5.6 that in 1979 Pope John Paul II named Francis of Assisi the patron saint of ecology.

In a recent work, Pope Benedict XVI says of creation that:

> Nature expresses a design of love and truth. *It is prior to us, and it has been given to us by God as the setting for our life. Nature speaks to us of the Creator and his love for humanity.* (2009, 55)

Additionally, the recent *Compendium of Catholic Social Teaching* also incorporates these insights about respect and care for the Earth. Chapter 10 of the *Compendium*, entitled "Safeguarding the Environment," discusses Biblical aspects of creation, the relationship between human beings and the environment, and how care for the environment is a common responsibility (2005, secs 451–487). The *Compendium* describes how nature is the work of God's creative action and "all beings are interdependent in the universal order established by the Creator" (secs 451–466).

Ethically, humanity is called to be a "co-operator with God in the work of creation" (sec 460). The world is a garden that God asks us to take care of; it is our "duty," and we must have "respect for other living creatures" (secs 451, 459). Simply viewing "the environment as 'resource' risks threatening the environment as 'home'" (sec 461). The *Compendium* explicitly says that

> *Franciscan spirituality in particular has witnessed to this sort of kinship of man with his creaturely environment, fostering in him an attitude of respect for every reality of the surrounding world. (sec 464)*

Another way to connect respect and care for the Earth to a Catholic and Franciscan ethic is by using the ethical principles from Catholic social teaching. Many of those principles apply here. I will focus on four of them. First, the *principle of the common good*, for example, which says there is a common good that humanity is responsible for ensuring and attaining, straightforwardly applies to how we behave toward the Earth (secs 160–184; see diagram 4.5).

As the *Compendium* explains:

> *Care for the environment represents a challenge for all of humanity. It is a matter of a common and universal duty, that of respecting a common good, destined for all. (sec 466)*

The common good, as something destined for all, connects very easily to a different principle, the *principle of the universal destination of goods*. According to that principle, the goods of the Earth were created by God to be used for all (secs 481–482, 484). Because of this, the goods of the Earth must be cared for and not be taken for granted, misused, or wasted. A good specific example here is water. Not only is safe drinking water necessary for the common good, and a natural resource to be used for all, but it is also a natural resource that "must be used rationally and in solidarity with others" (sec 485).

That water should be used "in solidarity with others," obviously weaves in the *principle of solidarity*: we must be determined to commit ourselves in solidarity to the good of all (secs 193–196; 476, 486–486; see diagram 4.5).

Access to safe drinking water might seem unimportant or insignificant, or something we routinely take for granted, misuse, or waste; yet as the *Compendium* points out:

> *Inadequate access to safe drinking water affects the well-being of a large number of people and is often the cause of disease, suffering, conflicts, poverty and even death. (sec 484)*

The *principle of the preferential option for the poor* is thus relevant here, since it asserts that the poor and marginalized should be the focus of particular concern (secs 182–184). Interestingly, four different principles of Catholic social teaching—the principle of the common good, the principle of the universal destination of goods, the principle of solidarity, and the principle of the preferential option for the poor, all converge on this one issue regarding care and respect for the Earth.

6.5 Conclusion

We started off this chapter by taking a look at the story of Francis and the wolf of Gubbio. We saw how the story illustrates how Francis sought to be a Christian peacemaker and how Francis regarded each member of God's creation as brother or sister. We then looked at ethical issues centering on caring for self, caring for other human beings, caring for others who are marginalized, and lastly caring for creation.

Drawing from Francis, Bonaventure, Scotus, and other resources from the Catholic tradition, we reviewed how Catholic Franciscan virtue and care ethics have many wide-ranging applications, from care of self, care of community, and care of creation.

This final chapter has not introduced any new ethical concepts, principles, or theories. It has simply tried to sum up, tie together, and illustrate how a Catholic and Franciscan ethics can apply to a wide variety of issues. By using the discussion questions at the end of this chapter you can continue to apply Catholic and Franciscan ethics to many, many more situations and issues than we have had time to look at in this chapter.

Pope John Paul II wrote the introduction to the *Catechism of the Catholic Church*, and there he stated that he hoped the new *Catechism* would encourage and assist in the writing of new local catechisms (1992, 6). I hope that *Catholic and Franciscan Ethics* (CFE) can serve as a local catechism for those who are seeking a concise introduction to the Catholic and Franciscan ethical traditions.

The picture on the cover of this book is of a small church that is located two and a half miles from Assisi, in Italy; a small chapel that Francis personally repaired and was later given to him.

Bonaventure, in his biography of Francis, tells the story of how one day when Francis was praying inside a different small chapel badly in need of repair, also close to Assisi, Francis believed that Jesus spoke to him from a crucifix and said, "Francis, go and build up My house, which, as thou seest, is falling into ruin" (1261, chp 2, 18). Francis decided to help repair the little church.

As was mentioned in section 5.1, Francis' father was a successful cloth merchant, and so to buy materials to repair the chapel Francis sold some of his father's cloth and gave the money to the priest who was the caretaker of the rundown chapel. Francis' father found out what Francis had done and was extremely angry. Francis' father tried to convince Francis to abandon his project, and when he could not convince him, he brought Francis to the Bishop of Assisi to force Francis to give up his inheritance and everything his father had given him.

Standing there in front of his father and the bishop, Francis took off his clothes and handed them to his father saying: "Until this hour I have called thee my father on earth; from henceforth, I may say confidently, *my Father Who art in heaven*, in Whose hands I have laid up all my treasures, all my trust, and all my hope'" (Bonaventure 1261, chp 2, 20). Having cut his ties with his biological father, Francis resumed his project of restoring the little church. When the church was repaired, he came across another church in need of repair and restored that one, too.

Bonaventure describes how when *that* church was restored, Francis

> came to a place called Portiuncula, where was a church ... which had been deserted, and which, for want of care, was now falling into decay. (Bonaventure 1261, chp 2, 24)

That third little church that Francis repaired came to be called *La Porziuncola*, and it is the little chapel pictured on the cover of this book; it is currently housed *inside* the larger St. Mary of the Angels church.

The picture provides a symbolic representation of the relationship between the Franciscan and Catholic traditions. Just as Francis' little chapel is today housed inside the large church of St. Mary of the Angels, the Franciscan ethical tradition is housed inside the larger Catholic ethical tradition.

Concepts, Principles, Theories, and Traditions Introduced in Chapter 6

None

Review Questions

1. How is the wolf of Gubbio story an ethical story? Explain how Francis' dealing with the wolf is consistent with the principle of the Golden Rule and the principle of charity.
2. What is meant by the title The Little Flowers of St. Francis of Assisi?
3. Do you think St. Francis makes a good role model? Why or why not?
4. In what ways did St. Francis exhibit care for self?
5. What does Bonaventure mean by "stages of illumination"?
6. What is meant by "the Franciscan dialogue approach"?
7. What does the phrase *pace e bene* mean, and what does it have to do with Franciscan ethics?
8. What does it mean to be a "marginalized" person?
9. What does Scotus mean by saying that the incarnation would have taken place even if humanity had not sinned?

Discussion Questions

1. At St. Bonaventure University, which is located in western New York, there is a tall tower on which hangs a large banner that says: "Thisness = Respect (for everyone and everything!)." Explain how this statement is an application of Scotus' concept.
2. Discuss care for self and smoking cigarettes.
3. Discuss abortion and respect and care for human life.
4. Another interesting example of the marginalized in today's society is the marginalized elderly (Pinckaers 1998, 45). In what ways do you personally have care and respect for the marginalized people of society?

5. Would Franciscans view recycling as something to be done out of duty or out of love? Explain.

6. In the document *Global Climate Change: A Plea for Dialogue, Prudence, and the Common Good* (2001), the United States Conference of Catholic Bishops says:

> *The virtue of prudence is paramount in addressing climate change. This virtue is not only a necessary one for individuals in leading morally good lives, but is also vital to the moral health of the larger community. Prudence is intelligence applied to our actions. It allows us to discern what constitutes the common good in a given situation. Prudence requires a deliberate and reflective process that aids in the shaping of the community's conscience. Prudence not only helps us identify the principles at stake in a given issue, but also moves us to adopt courses of action to protect the common good. Prudence is not, as popularly thought, simply a cautious and safe approach to decisions. Rather, it is a thoughtful, deliberate, and reasoned basis for taking or avoiding action to achieve a moral good.*

Which ethical concepts and ethical principles are they relying on to make their case?

Appendix 1
Catholic and Franciscan Ethical Concepts, Principles, And Theories

Catholic and Franciscan Ethical Concepts

care for the earth Attending to the needs of the Earth.

care for human life Attending to the needs of human beings.

care for the marginalized Attending to the needs of the marginalized.

care for self Attending to one's personal needs.

catechism A book that attempts to describe Church teachings. There have been several Catholic catechisms. The most recent one was published in 1992.

character The concept that each person possesses a distinctive grouping of traits (e.g., prudence, courage, and temperance).

command An order that directs us to perform an action; a prescription that prescribes what we ought to do.

common good The good of all. For Aquinas, every law should aim at it.

compendium A book that compiles a large amount of information. *The Compendium of Catholic Social Teaching* (2005) compiles the Catholic Church's social teachings.

dignity The value that a person has by simply being a person; a person's value, which ought to be respected by others.

divine law The revealed word of God that provides guidance as to how human beings can achieve eternal salvation.

duty Something that is required to do; a responsibility; an obligation.

eternal law God's plan as God understands it.

ethics Guidelines about how we should live, guidelines about right and wrong.

freedom The ability to make rational choices.

free will That which gives a being the ability to make rational choices.

grace Blessings given by God.

habit The concept that repeated actions eventually become second nature, because over time repeated actions will require less effort. A moral virtue is a good habit.

haecceity Literally, it means "thisness" (*haec* = "this"); it is Scotus' term for the special individuality that makes a singular thing what it is and differentiates it from all other things.

happiness, the good life A state of blessedness and contentment toward which all human beings strive.

human action A deed undertaken by a human person through the use of his or her freedom.

human goods Aquinas identifies four categories of fundamental human goods: life, procreation, sociability, and knowledge.

human law Laws that are designed, proposed, passed, and enacted by humans.

humility of the incarnation The incarnation is the act of God (the divine person of Jesus) taking on human form. The Franciscan tradition regards the incarnation as an indication of God's humility.

incarnation The act of God (the divine person of Jesus) taking on human form.

love (charity) The kind of love that Jesus commands; good will toward God and others.

manger Something one finds in a stable; a box that holds food for the animals to eat from. After Jesus was born, his mother Mary wrapped him and put him a manger, since Mary and Joseph were staying in a stable.

moral right A legitimate and rightful claim that a person has, even if he or she hasn't done anything. In the Catholic and Franciscan tradition, this kind of personal moral right should be acknowledged and recognized simply because a person is made in God's image and has dignity.

moral theology A systematic reflection on the way of life taught by one's religion.

moral virtue A character trait that contributes to one's happiness. Examples include prudence, courage, and temperance.

motive/intention An internal state of willing.

natural inclinations The concept that human nature directs human beings toward certain fundamental goods, which human beings then naturally value.

natural law The rational creature's participation in and (limited) understanding of the eternal law.

Nicene Creed A prayer/statement of belief created by the Catholic Church at the council at Nicaea in western Turkey in the year 325. It states the most important parts of the Catholic faith, and reciting it became a part of Christian worship.

obligation Something one is required to do; a responsibility; a duty.

Parable of the Good Samaritan A story with an ethical message that was told by Jesus and appears in the New Testament of the Bible.

person A human being made in the image and likeness of God.

philosophy Literally, it means "love of wisdom" (*philo* = "love," *sophy* = "wisdom"), and it is an activity of investigation that seeks true answers to basic questions about human beings and all of reality.

relational love According to Bonaventure, God is relational love, and human beings are called to enter into loving personal relationship with God.

right/wrong Very basic and general terms that describe what ought, and ought not, to be done.

role model One of the natural ways human beings learn is by imitating others. The concept of a role model is a person who possesses and thus displays developed character traits.

Second Vatican Council A very large meeting organized by the Catholic Church with the aim of renewing the life of the Church. It was held in Vatican City from the years 1962 to 1965.

should The guiding quality of ethics; equivalent to *ought.*

sin Turning away from God.

theological virtue A virtue that is not the result of habitual actions like a moral virtue is, but is instilled into human souls by God. Faith, hope, and charity (love) are theological virtues.

theology A systematic reflection on one's faith.

Trinity The concept that God is three persons in one: Father, Son, and Holy Spirit.

vice A character trait that stands in the way of achieving happiness.

virtue A character trait that contributes to one's happiness. Examples include prudence, courage, and temperance.

Catholic and Franciscan Ethical Principles

ought implies can A principle that clarifies what an obligation is. To say that you should (ought to, are obliged to) do something, presupposes that you are capable of doing it.

Pauline principle The ethical principle that says it is not morally permissible to do evil so that good may follow. (The end does not justify the means.)

personalist principle The Catholic social teaching principle that says the human person is made in the image of God and has dignity, and ought therefore be respected.

principle of charity Jesus' twofold commandment of love that says we should love God with all our hearts and love our neighbor as ourselves.

principle of the common good The Catholic social teaching principle that says there is a common good that humanity is responsible for safeguarding and managing.

principle of the Golden Rule The ethical principle that says you ought to do unto others as you would have them do unto you.

principle of natural law The ethical principle that says we ought to perform those actions that promote the values specified by the natural inclinations of human beings.

principle of participation The Catholic social teaching principle that says citizens should participate and contribute to the common good through political participation.

principle of the preferential option for the poor The Catholic social teaching principle that says the poor and marginalized should be the focus of particular concern.

principle of solidarity The Catholic social teaching principle that says we should be determined to commit ourselves in solidarity to the good of all.

principle of subsidiarity The Catholic social teaching principle that says a larger organization should help and allow subordinate organizations to achieve those tasks of which they are capable, without interference.

principle of the universal destination of goods The Catholic social teaching principle that says the earth and all it contains should be seen as destined for all peoples.

Catholic and Franciscan Ethical Theories and Traditions

action-centered ethics An approach to ethics that focuses on the morality of the action. To determine right from wrong, some action theories focus on the person's intention in performing the action; other action theories focus on the outcome or end of the action. Another way that action theories say to determine if an action is right or wrong is by using ethical principles.

care ethics The theory and tradition that views caring as the key ethical ideal; to live an ethical life is to care for those with whom we are in relationship.

Catholic Christian ethics tradition An ethical tradition derived from the Bible and developed through the reflection of Catholics over the course of many centuries.

Catholic social teaching An ethical teaching that the Catholic Church formulated and articulated in response to large societal changes that began to take place in the late nineteenth century.

Catholic and Franciscan ethical tradition The Catholic ethical tradition as it has been supported and enriched by St. Francis of Assisi and his followers.

deontological ethics (morality of obligation) The theory and tradition that focuses on ethical duties and says that actions are ethically right or wrong depending on whether they are in accord with one's ethical duties.

just war theory A theory that the Catholic tradition has formulated over many centuries that addresses the conditions under which killing in wartime may be ethically permissible.

natural law ethics The theory and tradition that says there are universal ethical standards discoverable through human reflection on human natural inclinations.

virtue-centered ethics The ethical theory and tradition that focuses on discovering which character traits are most important for living an ethically good life.

Appendix 2
Table of Catholic Social Teaching Documents and Their Ethical Components

Publication	Issues Discussed	Ethical Components Used
Pope Leo XIII, *Rerum Novarum* (1891)	The condition of workers: wages, hours required to work, health and safety standards in the workplace, child labor, worker associations; property, socialism; new systems in society, great wealth, many poor.	*Biblical*: Principles of Christian living as found in the Gospel. *Virtue ethics*: Virtue/vice, avarice, envy, pride, thrift, justice, injustice, prudence, mercy, charity, eternal reward. *Natural law ethics*: Aquinas, eternal law, natural law, divine law, human law. *Deontological ethics*: commandments, duties, rights, dignity.
Pope Pius XI, *Quadragesimo Anno* (1931)	The condition of workers: wages, associations, workplace conditions; private property, gap between non-owning workers and the very rich; socialism, communism.	*Biblical*: Divine revelation, law of the Gospel. *Virtue ethics*: Virtues, justice, injustice, charity, faith, greed, selfishness, courage, honesty, eternal salvation (supernatural happiness). *Natural law ethics*: Aquinas, natural law, moral law, divine law, human law, the common good. *Deontological ethics*: Commandments, duties, obligations, rights, right of private property/ownership, dignity, freedom.

(continued)

Publication	Issues Discussed	Ethical Components Used
Pope John XXIII, *Pacem in Terris* (1963)	Many independent nations; how citizens relate to their governments; minority citizens; political communities, the UN; interdependence of national economies; highly developed nations; developing nations; new weapons technologies, nuclear weapons; arms race; stockpiling of these weapons.	*Biblical*: Paul, Christian principles. *Virtue ethics*: Augustine, perfections, justice, prudence, charity, faith, solidarity, humility, pride, eternal salvation (supernatural happiness). *Natural law ethics*: Aquinas, natural law, law written in their hearts, universal common good, human law, eternal law. *Deontological ethics*: Person, free will, freedom, rights, duties, dignity, right to life, right to bodily integrity, right to the means necessary for the proper development of life, workers' rights, right to private property.
Pope Paul VI, *Populorum Progressio* (1967)	The poor, especially in developing countries, facing disease, hunger for food and education; authentic human development; work, profit, competition, economic progress; excessive economic and social inequalities between rich countries and poor nations.	*Biblical*: Gospel, Jesus in Matthew, Bible, St. Paul. *Virtue ethics*: Charity, faith, hope, salvation, solidarity, avarice, justice, injustice, self-mastery, courage, generosity, selfishness, pride. *Natural law ethics*: Common good, moral law, natural law. *Deontological ethics*: Freedom, responsibility, obligation, dignity, person, duties, rights, right to property, right to free commerce.
Pope Paul VI, *Octogesima Adveniens* (1971)	Inequalities between nations; urbanization; exploitation of nature, negative impact on the environment; a world dominated by scientific and technological change.	*Biblical*: Gospel, Gospel of John, Jesus. *Virtue ethics*: Justice, injustice, hope, charity, mercy, pride, humility, selfishness, solidarity, supernatural destiny (salvation). *Natural law ethics*: Moral law, common good. *Deontological ethics*: Responsibility, dignity, freedom, rights, person, duties.

Publication	Issues Discussed	Ethical Components Used
Pope John Paul II, *Laborem Exercens* (1981)	Human work; developments in technological, economic, and political conditions; cost of energy; pollution of nature; family life.	*Biblical*: Genesis, Gospel, Christ, parables, St. Paul. *Virtue ethics*: Justice, injustice, faith, solidarity, industriousness, transcendent destiny. *Natural law ethics*: Aquinas, common good. *Deontological ethics*: Rights, dignity, person, freedom, obligation, duty, right to private property, right to common use.
Pope John Paul II, *Sollicitudo Rei Socialis* (1987)	Development/underdevelopment of peoples; obstacles to authentic human development; the UN; unequal distribution of world resources; consumerism.	*Biblical*: Genesis, Christ, parables, Gospel, St. Paul. *Virtue ethics*: Virtues, solidarity, justice, injustice, faith, selfishness, charity, mercy. *Natural law ethics*: Common good. *Deontological ethics*: Ten Commandments, duty, obligation, responsibility, rights, dignity, person, freedom, right to private property.
Pope John Paul II, *Centesimus Annus* (1991)	Collapse of some dictatorships; abandonment of communism; democracy, totalitarianism, fundamentalism; property, material goods, land, natural resources, ownership, capitalism, free markets, business, profit, monopolies, the government's role; poor countries in debt to richer countries; use of drugs; destruction of natural environment, consumerism; war; globalization.	*Biblical*: Genesis, Christ, Gospel, parable, scripture, Divine Revelation. *Virtue ethics*: Virtues, justice, injustice, solidarity (friendship), charity, faith, diligence, industriousness, prudence, courage, patience, selfishness, eternal salvation. *Natural law ethics*: Aquinas, common good. *Deontological ethics*: Person, dignity, duty, responsibility, obligations, freedom, right, right to private property, right to a just wage.

(continued)

Publication	Issues Discussed	Ethical Components Used
Pope Benedict XVI, *Caritas in Veritate* (2009)	Globalization; authentic human development; technological and economic development and progress; world hunger, food insecurity; commercial relationships, economic activity, stakeholders. different types of businesses; population growth; nonrenewable energy sources; humanity's relationship to the natural environment.	*Biblical*: Genesis, Christ, Gospel, John, Paul, Divine revelation. *Virtue ethics*: Augustine, virtues, charity, principle of charity, courage, generosity, justice, faith, hope, humility, solidarity, selfishness, honesty, happiness/salvation. *Natural law ethics*: Natural law, moral law, law etched on human hearts, the common good. *Deontological ethics*: Command, duties, responsibility, rights, rights to life, freedom, dignity, person.

Appendix 3

The Canticle of the Creatures (1225)

Most High, all-powerful, good Lord,
　　Yours are the praises, the glory, and the honor, and all blessing.
To You alone, Most High, do they belong.
　　and no human is worthy to mention Your name.
Praise be You, my Lord, with all Your creatures
　　especially Sir Brother Sun, who is the day
　　and through whom You give us light.
And he is beautiful and radiant with great splendor;
　　and bears a likeness of You, Most High One.
Praised be You, my Lord, through Sister Moon
　　and the stars; in heaven You formed them clear and precious and beautiful.
Praised be You, my Lord, through Brother wind,
　　and through the air, cloudy and serene, and every kind of weather,
　　through whom You give sustenance to Your creatures.
Praise be You, my Lord, through Sister Water,
　　who is very useful and humble and precious and chaste.
Praise be You, my Lord, through Brother Fire,
　　through whom You light the night,
　　and he is beautiful and playful and robust and strong.
Praised be You, my Lord, through our Sister
Mother Earth, who sustains us and governs us,
　　and who produces various fruit with colored flowers and herbs.
Praise be You, my Lord, through those who give pardon for Your love,
　　and bear infirmity and tribulation.
Blessed are those who endure in peace
　　for by You, Most High, shall they be crowned.
Praise be you, my Lord, through our Sister Bodily Death,
　　from whom no one living can escape. Woe to those who die in mortal sin.

Blessed are those whom death will find in Your most holy will,
    for the second death shall do them no harm.
Praise and bless my Lord and give him thanks
    and serve Him with great humility.

Appendix 4

Suggested Readings

Introduction

The "Prayer Before the Crucifix" is also known as the "Prayer for Enlightenment" (see Noonan and Gasnick 1987, 15).

Chapter 1. Ancient Catholic Ethics

The Parable of the Good Samaritan is from the Gospel of Luke, Chp 10, verses 25–37, and it, along with all passages from the Bible quoted in *CFE*, is taken from *The New American Bible* (1990).

The *Catechism* calls the Ten Commandments "the Decalogue" (sec 2056) and says that the Ten Commandments express our fundamental duties toward God and neighbor (sec 2072). Sections 2084–2557 of the *Catechism* offer an in-depth analysis of the Ten Commandments, unpacking how they relate to many aspects of human living. The *Catechism* (sec 2514), when introducing the discussion of the ninth commandment, lists Jesus' restatement of the sixth commandment: "Every one who looks at a woman lustfully has already committed adultery with her in his heart" (Matthew 5:28). Due to their subject matter, the sixth and ninth commandments are importantly linked.

For more on *command* as an important ethical concept, see the collection of articles in Helm (1981).

The *Catechism* says "The Beatitudes are at the heart of Jesus' preaching" (sec 1716). The concept of the supernatural is also mentioned in the *Catechism*: "beatitude surpasses the understanding and powers of man. It comes from an entirely free gift of God: whence it is called *supernatural*" (secs 1722, 1727). The *Catechism* describes how the Sermon on the Mount "does not add new external precepts, but proceeds to reform the heart, the root of human acts, where man chooses between the pure and the impure, where faith, hope, and charity are formed and with them the other virtues" (sec 1968).

The view that God is not only a creator and commander but love itself is of such significant importance in the Catholic tradition that Pope Benedict XVI entitled the first encyclical letter of his pontificate *God Is Love* (2006). As an ethical principle, the principle of charity is a twofold yet single commandment of love (*Catechism,* sec 2055; see secs 2083 and 2196). The *Catechism* says: "all the works of perfect Christian virtue spring from love and have no other objective than to arrive at love" (sec 25).

As an ethical principle, the Golden Rule "helps one discern, in concrete situations, whether or not it would be appropriate to reveal the truth to someone who asks for it" (*Catechism,* sec. 2510).

The Pauline principle is stated in the *Catechism* (secs 1753, 1755–1756, 1759, 1789); there it is not called the Pauline principle, but is simply unnamed. The *Catechism* states the principle in two different ways: "The end does not justify the means" and "One may not do evil so that good may result from it." For more about the ethical theory of virtue ethics, see Aristotle (337 BCE), MacIntyre (1981), Crisp and Slote (1997), and Gupta (2002, part IV). For Christian ethics in particular, see Hauerwas and Pinches (1997). Zabzebski (1998, 544) in her work strives to "give the traditional Christian idea of ethics as the imitation of Christ a theoretical structure." For more on happiness as part of Christian ethics, see Wadell (2012).

About the human ability to know God and God's law, see the *Catechism* (secs 35–38, 1954–1956); also see Pope John Paul II's work *Faith and Reason* (1998).

Chapter 2. Medieval Catholic Ethics

The Nicene Creed was created at the Council of Nicaea (325). The definition of theology as a systematic reflection on one's faith is from Placher (1983, 12). The definition of moral theology as a systematic reflection on the way of life that Jesus taught is from McCarthy (1984, 27). The *Catechism* quotes Augustine's *Commentary on the Sermon on the Mount* where Augustine says the Sermon is the perfect way of the Christian life and contains all the precepts needed to shape one's life (sec 1966). The *Catechism* describes how the Beatitudes respond to the natural desire for happiness, and it quotes St. Augustine on this point (sec 1718).

These are the Biblical and *Catechism* references to both God and humans having freedom: Revelation 4:11 and CCC sections 295, 1700, 1704–1705, and 1730–1731.

In the *Catechism* in the section on the fifth commandment, the conditions for a just war—according to just war theory—are listed (sec 2309).

Aquinas also calls human law by a different name: *positive law* (1274, I-II, Q92, article 2). In that section Aquinas discusses how human law becomes problematic when it conflicts with natural law. Augustine does not use the term *human law*; Augustine calls it *temporal law* (387, book 1, verse 6). The *Catechism* outlines the different kinds of law in sections 1951–1952. See also the whole section on the moral law: part 3, section 1, chapter 3.

Aquinas clarifies that "Although charity is love, not all love is charity" (1274 I-II, Q62, article 2). For a short, critical introduction to Aquinas' ethical thought, see O'Connor (1967). For a recent application of just war theory to nuclear warfare, see National Conference of Catholic Bishops (1983, 26–34).

Chapter 3. Modern Catholic Ethics

This chapter relies on Pinckaers (1995, chp 11; 2001, chp 4). About the Sermon on the Mount being interpreted to be about spirituality and not ethics, and the modern manuals' omission of the Sermon, see Pinckaers (1995, 134–137). Pinckaers (1995, 262–263) says happiness was not included in the manuals.

For more about deontological ethics, see Kant (1785); Baron, Pettit, and Slote (1997); and Kagan (1998, chp 7).

The Catholic belief that God has freedom and humans have freedom, too, is found in several sources: the Bible (Revelation 4:11) and the *Catechism* (secs 295, 1700, 1704–1705, 1730–1731). In addition to Francisco Suárez, another early modern theologian who worked with natural law ethics and developed the modern sense of "moral right" is Francis de Vitoria (1483–1546). See Araujo (2012) and Brust (2012). The *Compendium* says that John XXIII's *Pacem in Terris* was the most in-depth discussion of human rights (sec 95).

Chapter 4. Contemporary Catholic Ethics

For the history of Catholic social teaching, see the Pontifical Council for Justice and Peace publication *Compendium of the Social Doctrine of the Church* (2005, chp 2) and the *Catechism* (secs 2419–2449).

The *Catechism* explains that the Ten Commandments must be interpreted in the light of the principle of charity (sec 2055). The Decalogue contains a privileged expression of the natural law (sec 2070).

The relationship between the Second Vatican Council and the *Catechism* is described in John Paul II (1992) and DiNoia et al. (1996, chp 2). For the relationship between the Council of Trent and *The Roman Catechism*, see Kevane (1985).

The *Catechism* says the practice of all the virtues is animated and inspired by charity (sec 1827). The *Catechism* says charity is a special virtue also because with faith and hope it is infused by God into human souls (sec 1813).

Chapter 5. Catholic Franciscan Ethics

For a history of the Franciscan tradition, see Osborne (1994). About the Franciscan tradition, Osborne says: "Since the end of the thirteenth century … there has been a form of theology called 'Franciscan.' The roots of this tradition are present in the New Testament, in the Church Fathers and in early, pre-thirteenth-century medieval theologians" (2003, 41).

The story of the manger scene in Greccio is from Celano (1229, chp 30), who was the first person to write a biography of St. Francis of Assisi. The phrase "humility of the incarnation" appears in Celano (1229, Bk I, chp 30). Guinan (2006, 30) argues that "many of Francis's favorite texts and images of Christ derive from" the Gospel of John. Delio (2003, 11) says that it took Francis a lifetime to develop Christian attitudes and behaviors. Pinckaers (1998) spells out the connections among the Beatitudes, virtues, and happiness. McMichael (2012, 133) says that "much of spirit of the Sermon on the Mount can be found in the writings of Francis." Nothwehr (2005, 16) describes Francis' attitude toward death. For more detailed examination of Francis' spirituality as derived from the Bible, see Van Den Goorbergh and Zweerman (2001, 2007).

About Francis' travels to the Middle East, see *Little Flowers* (Alger 1390, chp 24), Warren (2003), and Hoeberichts (1997). In meeting with the

Sultan, McMichael says that Francis' "goal was to preach the Gospel of Christ and bring non-believers to the fullness of the Christian faith" (2012, 137).

For examples of theories of care ethics, see Noddings (1984) and Held (2006). Pinckaers (2001, chp 6) describes the importance of understanding the Christian concept of happiness in terms of spiritual joy. With regard to the concept of *role model* in Franciscan virtue ethics, Wolter and O'Neill (1993, 84) say that "Example has always been a Franciscan way of influencing others. If reform is needed, it must begin with oneself. And we need to examine prayerfully our own life style." This notion also ties in with a saying attributed to Francis: "Preach the Gospel always. When necessary, use words." Francis advised his brothers to "preach by their deeds" (1221, chp 17).

The growth of the Franciscans from twelve to thirty thousand is described by Osborne (2003, 31). Saint Clare of Assisi (1194–1253) was one of the first followers of Saint Francis. She went on to found the Order of Poor Ladies, a religious order for women in the Franciscan tradition. For a glimpse into Clare's writings, see Van Den Goorbergh and Zweerman (2000).

According to Boehner (2002, 9), of all Bonaventure's writings the one most "deeply impregnated with the spirit of Saint Francis" is Bonaventure's *Itinerarium Mentis in Deum* ("Journey of the Mind to God"), which was published in 1259.

According to Johnson (2012, 144), Francis "proclaims that God's original declaration regarding the goodness of creation found in Genesis I: 31 has not been totally erased by the tragedy of sin." Thomas of Celano (1229, Book I, chp 29) notes the connection between Francis and his "Canticle" and the passage from the book of Daniel (3:52–81).

We can consider Scotus' teaching about haecceity as offering a solution to the philosophical problem of personal identity, which is a grouping of philosophical questions that asks: What makes you a particular person, different from others? Do you remain the same person over time? What makes you the same person over time? Scotus is also famous for his defense of the Immaculate Conception of Mary. In 1854 Pope Pius IX officially endorsed as correct Scotus' claims about the Immaculate Conception of Mary that he made in about 1304, that at the first moment of her conception Mary was free from original sin.

For a view critical of Francis' ethic of love, see Blanshard (1961, chp 3, "St Francis and the Supremacy of Feeling"). Blanshard overlooks that care for self includes reflection, and that pleasure and joy can come from prayer.

Loehr (2014, x) describes how Pope Francis took his name in honor of Saint Francis of Assisi.

Chapter 6. Catholic Franciscan Ethics: Some Applications

The deeper ethical meaning of the story of Francis and the wolf of Gubbio is in Blow (2003, unit 9). What Bonaventure says about light and illumination fits nicely with the importance that Francis places on brother sun in his "Canticle."

For a collection of articles on Franciscan thought and the environment, see Nothwehr (2002). Koenig-Bricker (2009, 8) says that Pope Benedict XVI has become "the 'greenest' Pope in history, by putting his words into practice ... in 2007 the Vatican became the world's first carbon-neutral country."

Through his writings we can see that Francis was committed to traditional Catholic beliefs, yet several aspects of his approach make him an appealing figure even far beyond the Catholic tradition (Dunstan 2012, 277). Francis' stance with regard to nature, his concern for the poor, and his example of how to dialogue with other faith traditions are factors that contribute to his wide appeal (Dunstan 2012, 276, 279–280, 284–285).

The Franciscan attitude of "let me share with you what has brought meaning to my life" is described in Blow (2003, unit 8, 5). Martin Luther King, Jr. is an example of someone who "exemplifies the Franciscan art of peacemaking through non-violence" (Blow 2003, unit 9, 8); see especially, King (1963), "Loving Your Enemies."

For more on Christian peacemaking, which includes discussion of just war theory, see Stanton-Rich (1987).

Appendix 5

Glossary

action-centered ethics An approach to ethics that focuses on the morality of the action. To determine right from wrong, some action theories focus on the person's intention in performing the action; other action theories focus on the outcome or end of the action. Another way that action theories say to determine if an action is right or wrong is by using ethical principles.

care ethics The theory and tradition that views caring as the key ethical ideal; to live an ethical life is to care for those with whom we are in relationship.

care for the earth Attending to the needs of the Earth. (A concept.)

care for human life Attending to the needs of human beings. (A concept.)

care for the marginalized Attending to the needs of the marginalized. (A concept.)

care for self Attending to one's personal needs. (A concept.)

catechism A book that attempts to describe Church teachings. There have been several Catholic catechisms. The most recent one was published in 1992.

Catholic Christian ethics tradition An ethical tradition derived from the Bible and developed through the reflection of Catholics over the course of many centuries.

Catholic social teaching An ethical teaching that the Catholic Church formulated and articulated in response to large societal changes that began to take place in the late nineteenth century.

Catholic and Franciscan ethical tradition The Catholic ethical tradition as it has been supported and enriched by St. Francis of Assisi and his followers.

character The concept that each person possesses a distinctive grouping of traits (e.g., prudence, courage, and temperance).

command An order that directs us to perform an action; a prescription that prescribes what we ought to do. (A concept.)

common good The good of all. For Aquinas, every law should aim at it. (A concept.)

compendium A book that compiles a large amount of information. *The Compendium of Catholic Social Teaching* (2005) compiles the Catholic Church's social teachings.

deontological ethics (morality of obligation) The theory and tradition that focuses on ethical duties and says that actions are ethically right or wrong depending on whether they are in accord with one's ethical duties.

dignity The value that a person has by simply being a person; a person's value, which ought to be respected by others. (A concept.)

divine law The revealed word of God that provides guidance as to how human beings can achieve eternal salvation. (A concept.)

duty Something that is required to do; a responsibility; an obligation. (A concept.)

eternal law God's plan as God understands it. (A concept.)

ethics Guidelines about how we should live, guidelines about right and wrong.

freedom The ability to make rational choices. (A concept.)

free will That which gives a being the ability to make rational choices. (A concept.)

grace Blessings given by God. (A concept.)

habit The concept that repeated actions eventually become second nature, because over time repeated actions will require less effort. A moral virtue is a good habit.

haecceity Literally, it means "thisness" (*haec* = "this"); it is Scotus' term for the special individuality that makes a singular thing what it is and differentiates it from all other things. (A concept.)

happiness, the good life A state of blessedness and contentment toward which all human beings strive. (A concept.)

human action A deed undertaken by a human person through the use of his or her freedom. (A concept.)

human goods Aquinas identifies four categories of fundamental human goods: life, procreation, sociability, and knowledge. (A concept.)

human law Laws that are designed, proposed, passed, and enacted by humans. (A concept.)

humility of the incarnation The incarnation is the act of God (the divine person of Jesus) taking on human form. The Franciscan tradition regards the incarnation as an indication of God's humility. (A concept.)

incarnation The act of God (the divine person of Jesus) taking on human form. (A concept.)

just war theory A theory that the Catholic tradition has formulated over many centuries that addresses the conditions under which killing in wartime may be ethically permissible.

love (charity) The kind of love that Jesus commands; good will toward God and others. (A concept.)

manger Something one finds in a stable; a box that holds food for the animals to eat from. After Jesus was born, his mother Mary wrapped him and put him a manger, since Mary and Joseph were staying in a stable.

moral right A legitimate and rightful claim that a person has, even if he or she hasn't done anything. In the Catholic and Franciscan tradition, this kind of personal moral right should be acknowledged and recognized simply because a person is made in God's image and has dignity.

moral theology A systematic reflection on the way of life taught by one's religion.

moral virtue A character trait that contributes to one's happiness. Examples include prudence, courage, and temperance. (A concept.)

motive/intention An internal state of willing. (A concept.)

natural inclinations The concept that human nature directs human beings toward certain fundamental goods, which human beings then naturally value.

natural law The rational creature's participation in and (limited) understanding of the eternal law. (A concept.)

natural law ethics The theory and tradition that says there are universal ethical standards discoverable through human reflection on human natural inclinations.

Nicene Creed A prayer/statement of belief created by the Catholic Church at the council at Nicaea in western Turkey in the year 325. It states the most important parts of the Catholic faith, and reciting it became a part of Christian worship

obligation Something one is required to do; a responsibility; a duty. (A concept.)

ought implies can A principle that clarifies what an obligation is. To say that you should (ought to, are obliged to) do something presupposes that you are capable of doing it. (A principle.)

Parable of the Good Samaritan A story with an ethical message that was told by Jesus and appears in the New Testament of the Bible.

Pauline principle The ethical principle that says it is not morally permissible to do evil so that good may follow. (The end does not justify the means.)

person A human being made in the image and likeness of God. (A concept.)

personalist principle The Catholic social teaching principle that says the human person is made in the image of God and has dignity, and ought therefore be respected.

philosophy Literally, it means "love of wisdom" (*philo* = "love," *sophy* = "wisdom"), and it is an activity of investigation that seeks true answers to basic questions about human beings and all of reality.

principle of charity Jesus' twofold commandment of love that says we should love God with all our hearts and love our neighbor as ourselves. (A principle.)

principle of the common good The Catholic social teaching principle that says there is a common good that humanity is responsible for safeguarding and managing.

principle of the Golden Rule The ethical principle that says you ought to do unto others as you would have them do unto you.

principle of natural law The ethical principle that says we ought to perform those actions that promote the values specified by the natural inclinations of human beings.

principle of participation The Catholic social teaching principle that says citizens should participate and contribute to the common good through political participation.

principle of the preferential option for the poor The Catholic social teaching principle that says the poor and marginalized should be the focus of particular concern.

principle of solidarity The Catholic social teaching principle that says we should be determined to commit ourselves in solidarity to the good of all.

principle of subsidiarity The Catholic social teaching principle that says a larger organization should help and allow subordinate organizations to achieve those tasks of which they are capable, without interference.

principle of the universal destination of goods The Catholic social teaching principle that says the earth and all it contains should be seen as destined for all peoples.

relational love According to Bonaventure, God is relational love, and human beings are called to enter into loving personal relationship with God. (A concept.)

right/wrong Very basic and general terms that describe what ought, and ought not, to be done. (Concepts.)

role model One of the natural ways human beings learn is by imitating others. The concept of a role model is a person who possesses and thus displays developed character traits.

Second Vatican Council A very large meeting organized by the Catholic Church with the aim of renewing the life of the Church. It was held in Vatican City from the years 1962 to 1965.

should The guiding quality of ethics; equivalent to *ought*. (A concept.)

sin Turning away from God. (A concept.)

theological virtue A virtue that is not the result of habitual actions, like a moral virtue is, but is instilled into human souls by God. Faith, hope, and charity (love) are theological virtues. (A concept.)

theology A systematic reflection on one's faith.

Trinity The concept that God is three persons in one: Father, Son, and Holy Spirit.

vice A character trait that stands in the way of achieving happiness. (A concept.)

virtue A character trait that contributes to one's happiness. Examples include prudence, courage, and temperance. (A concept.)

virtue-centered ethics The ethical theory and tradition that focuses on discovering which character traits are most important for living an ethically good life.

Appendix 6

References

Alexander of Hales. 1240. *Summa theologica*. Collegium S. Bonaventurae, Quarracchi.

Alger, Abby Langdon (trans.). (1390) 1951. *The Little Flowers of St. Francis of Assisi*. Chicago: Henry Regnery Co.

Anselm of Canterbury. (1075) 2007. *The Devotions of Saint Anselm*. Whitefish, MT: Kessinger Publishing.

Aquinas, St. Thomas. (1264) 1945. *On the Truth of the Catholic Faith: Summa Contra Gentiles*. In *Basic Writings of Saint Thomas Aquinas, Vol Two*. New York: Random House.

———. (1274) 1989. *Summa Theologiae*. Translated by T. McDermott. Allen, TX: Christian Classics.

Araujo, Robert John. 2012. "Our Debt to De Vitoria: A Catholic Foundation of Human Rights," *Ave Maria Law Review* 10: 313–29.

Aristotle. (337 BCE) 1985. *Nicomachean Ethics*. Translated by T. Irwin. Indianapolis, IN: Hackett Publishing Co.

Augustine. (387) 1993. *On Free Choice of the Will*. Translated by T. Williams. Indianapolis, IN: Hackett Publishing Co.

———. (388) 2005. *The Morals of the Catholic Church*. Whitefish, MT: Kessinger Publishing.

———. (397) 1997. *The Confessions*. Translated by M. Boulding. New York: Vintage Books.

———. (413) 1977. *The City of God*. Translated by H. Bettenson. New York: Penguin Books.

———. (421) 1993. *The Enchiridion on Faith, Hope and Love*. Edited by Henry Paolucci. Washington, DC: Regnery Gateway.

Azor, Juan. (1602) [2013]. *Institutiones Morales*. RareBooksClub.com.

Baron, Marcia W., Philip Pettit, and Michael Slote. 1997. *Three Methods of Ethics: A Debate*. Malden, MA: Blackwell Publishers.

Blanshard, Brand. 1961. *Reason and Goodness*. London: George Allen & Unwin.

Blow, Thomas. 2003. *Build with Living Stones: Formation for Franciscan Life and Work*, 3rd ed. St. Bonaventure, NY: The Franciscan Institute.

Boehner, Philotheus. 2002. Introduction. In *Itinerarium Mentis in Deum (Journey of the Mind to God)*, translated by Z. Hayes, 9–32. Saint Bonaventure, NY: The Franciscan Institute.

Bonaventure. (1257) 1963. *The Breviloquium*. Translated by J. de Vinck. Paterson, NJ: St. Anthony Guild Press.

———. (1259) 2002. *Itinerarium Mentis in Deum (Journey of the Mind to God)*. Translated by Z. Hayes. Saint Bonaventure, NY: The Franciscan Institute.

———. (1260) 1960. *On the Perfection of Life*. In *Mystical Opuscula*, translated by J. de Vinck, 207–55. Paterson, NJ: St. Anthony Guild Press.

———. (1261) 1988. *The Life of St. Francis of Assisi*. Rockford, IL: Tan Books and Publishers.

———. (1267) 1995. *Collations on the Ten Commandments*. Translated by P. J. Spaeth. St. Bonaventure, NY: The Franciscan Institute.

Brust, Steven J. 2012. "Retrieving a Catholic Tradition of Subjective Natural Rights from the Late Scholastic Francisco Suarez, S.J." *Ave Maria Law Review* 10: 343–63.

Catholic Church. (1992) 1995. *Catechism of the Catholic Church*. New York: Doubleday.

Celano, Thomas of. (1229) 1999. *The Life of Saint Francis*. In Vol. I of *Francis of Assisi: Early Documents*, edited by R. J. Armstrong, J. A. W. Hellman, and W. J. Short. New York: New City Press.

———. (1247) 2000. *The Second Life of Saint Francis* [The Remembrance of the Desire of a Soul]. In Vol. II of *Francis of Assisi: Early Documents*, edited by R. J. Armstrong, J. A. W. Hellman, and W. J. Short. New York: New City Press.

Chesteron, G. K. 1923. *Saint Francis of Assisi*, in Gasnick 1980, 40–41.

Chinnici, Joseph P. 2003. "General Editor's Introduction," in Osborne 2003, v–xiii.

Crisp, Roger, and Michael Slote. (eds.) 1997. *Virtue Ethics*. New York: Oxford University Press.

Delio, Ilia. 2003. *A Franciscan View of Creation: Learning to Live in a Sacramental World*. St. Bonaventure, NY: The Franciscan Institute.

————, Keith Douglas Warner, and Pamela Wood. 2008. *Care for Creation*. Cincinnati, OH: St. Anthony Messenger Press.

Dennis, Marie, Joseph Nangle, Cynthia Moe-Lobeda, and Stuart Taylor. 1993. *St. Francis and the Foolishness of God*. Maryknoll, NY: Orbis Books.

Dignitatis Humanae. 1965. In Documents of Vatican II, 675–96.

DiNoia, J. Augustine, Gabriel O'Donnell, Romanus Cesario, and Peter John Cameron. 1996. *The Love That Never Ends: A Key to the Catechism of the Catholic Church*. Huntington, IN: Our Sunday Visitor.

Documents of Vatican II. 1966. Edited by Walter M. Abbott. New York: Guild Press.

Duns Scotus, John. (1298) 2005. *Early Oxford Lecture on Individuation*. Translated by A. B. Wolter. St. Bonaventure, NY: The Franciscan Institute.

————. (1300) 1987. *Opus Oxoniense*. In *Duns Scotus: Philosophical Writings*, translated by A. B. Wolter. Indianapolis, IN: Hackett.

————. (1302a) 1997. *Ordinatio*. In *Duns Scotus on the Will and Morality*, translated by A. B. Wolter. Indianapolis, IN: Hackett.

————. (1302b) 2001. *Ordinatio*. In *John Duns Scotus' Political and Economic Philosophy*, translated by A. B. Wolter. St. Bonaventure, NY: The Franciscan Institute.

Dunstan, Petà. 2012. "The Ecumenical Appeal of Francis." In *The Cambridge Companion to Francis of Assisi*, edited by M. J. P. Robson, 273–87. New York: Cambridge University.

Francis, Saint. (1205) 1999. "Prayer before the Crucifix." In Vol. I of *Francis of Assisi: Early Documents*, edited by R. J. Armstrong, J. A. W. Hellman, and W. J. Short, 40. New York: New City Press.

————. (1221) 1999. "The Earlier Rule." In Vol. I of *Francis of Assisi: Early Documents*, edited by R. J. Armstrong, J. A. W. Hellman, and W. J. Short, 63–86. New York: New City Press.

————. (1223) 1999. "The Later Rule." In Vol. I of *Francis of Assisi: Early Documents*, edited by R. J. Armstrong, J. A. W. Hellman, and W. J. Short, 99–106. New York: New City Press.

————. (1225) 1999. "Canticle of the Creatures." In Vol. I of *Francis of Assisi: Early Documents*, edited by R. J. Armstrong, J. A. W. Hellman, and W. J. Short, 113–14. New York: New City Press.

Gasnick, Roy M. (ed.). 1980. *The Francis Book: 800 Years with the Saint from Assisi*. New York: Macmillan Publishing.

Gaudium et Spes. 1965. In Documents of Vatican II, 199–308.

Guinan, Michael D. 2006. *The Franciscan Vision and the Gospel of John*. Saint Bonaventure, NY: The Franciscan Institute.

Gupta, Bina. (ed.). 2002. *Ethical Questions: East and West*. Lanham, MD: Rowman & Littlefield.

Hauerwas, Stanley, and Charles Pinches. 1997. *Christians among the Virtues*. Notre Dame, IN: University of Notre Dame Press.

Held, Virginia. 2006. *The Ethics of Care: Personal, Political, and Global*. New York: Oxford University Press.

Helm, Paul. (ed.). 1981. *Divine Commands and Morality*. New York: Oxford University Press.

Hoeberichts, J. 1997. *Francis and Islam*. Quincy, IL: Franciscan Press.

Ingham, Mary Beth. 1995. "A Certain Affection for Justice," in Nothwehr 2002: 325–33.

———. 2003. *Scotus for Dunces: An Introduction to the Subtle Doctor*. Saint Bonaventure, NY: The Franciscan Institute.

———. 2012. *The Harmony of Goodness: Mutuality and Moral Living According to John Duns Scotus*. Saint Bonaventure, NY: Franciscan Institute Publications.

——— and Thomas A. Shannon. 1993. *The Ethical Method of John Duns Scotus*. St. Bonaventure, NY: The Franciscan Institute.

Johnson, Timothy J. 2012. "Francis and Creation." In *The Cambridge Companion to Francis of Assisi*, edited by M. J. P. Robson, 143–58. New York: Cambridge University Press.

Kagan, Shelly. 1998. *Normative Ethics*. Boulder, CO: Westview Press.

Kant, Immanuel. (1785) 1981. *Grounding for the Metaphysics of Morals*. Translated by J. W. Ellington. Indianapolis, IN: Hackett Publishing Co.

Kevane, Eugene. 1985. "Introduction." In *The Roman Catechism*, i–xv. Boston, MA: St. Paul Editions.

King, Martin Luther, Jr. 1963. *Strength to Love*. Philadelphia: Fortress Press.

Koenig-Bricker, Woodene. 2009. *Ten Commandments for the Environment: Pope Benedict XVI Speaks Out for Creation and Justice*. Notre Dame, IN: Ave Maria Press.

Loehr, Gina. 2014. *Saint Francis, Pope Francis: A Common Vision*. Cincinnati, OH: Servant Books.

Massimi, Massimo. (1937) 1943. *Catholic Morality: Fundamentals and Summary*. Translated by J. I. Schade. Paterson, NJ: St. Anthony Guild Press.

McCarthy, Donald G. 1984. *Moral Theology Today: Certitudes and Doubts*. St. Louis, MO: The Pope John Center.

MacIntyre, Alasdair. 1981. *After Virtue*. Notre Dame, IN: University of Notre Dame Press.

McMichael, Steven J. 2012. "Francis and the Encounter with the Sultan (1219)." In *The Cambridge Companion to Francis of Assisi*, edited by M. J. P. Robson, 127–42. New York: Cambridge University Press.

National Conference of Catholic Bishops. 1983. *The Challenge of Peace: God's Promise and Our Response*. Washington, DC: United States Catholic Conference.

Noddings, Nel. 1984. *Caring: A Feminine Approach to Ethics & Moral Education*. Berkeley, CA: University of California Press.

Noonan, Hugh, and Roy M. Gasnick. 1987. *Francis of Assisi: The Song Goes On*. Cincinnati, OH: St. Anthony Messenger Press.

Nothwehr, Dawn M. (ed.). 2002. *Franciscan Theology of the Environment*. St. Quincy, IL: Franciscan Press.

———. 2005. *The Franciscan View of the Human Person*. St. Bonaventure, NY: The Franciscan Institute.

O'Connor, D. J. 1967. *Aquinas and Natural Law*. London: Macmillan.

Osborne, Kenan B. (ed.). (1994) 2007. *The History of Franciscan Theology*. St. Bonaventure, NY: The Franciscan Institute.

———. 2003. *The Franciscan Intellectual Tradition*. St. Bonaventure, NY: The Franciscan Institute.

Pinckaers, Servais. 1995. *The Sources of Christian Ethics*. Translated by M. T. Noble. Washington, DC: Catholic University of America.

———. 1998. *The Pursuit of Happiness—God's Way: Living the Beatitudes*. New York: Alba House.

———. 2001. *Morality: The Catholic View*. Translated by M. Sherwin. South Bend, IN: St. Augustine's Press.

Placher, William C. 1983. *A History of Christian Theology*. Philadelphia: Westminster Press.

Pontifical Council for Justice and Peace. 2005. *Compendium of the Social Doctrine of the Church*. Washington, DC: United States Conference of Catholic Bishops.

Pope Benedict XVI. 2006. *God Is Love*. Washington, DC: United States Conference of Catholic Bishops.

———. 2007. Message for the Celebration of the World Day of Peace. http://www.vatican.va/holy_father/benedict_xvi/messages/peace/documents/hf_ben-xvi_mes_20061208_xl-world-day-peace_en.html

———. 2009. *Charity in Truth (Caritas in Veritate)*. Washington, DC: United States Conference of Catholic Bishops.

———. 2010. *The Virtues*. Huntington, IN: Our Sunday Visitor.

———. 2011. *Great Teachers*. Huntington, IN: Our Sunday Visitor.

Pope John XXIII. 1963. *Pacem in Terris*. http://www.vatican.va/holy_father/john_xxiii/encyclicals/documents/hf_j-xxiii_enc_11041963_pacem_en.html

Pope John Paul II. 1978. *L'Osservatore Romano*, November 13, 1978, in Gasnick 1980, 8–9.

———. 1979. Apostolic Letter, *Inter Sanctos*. http://www.vatican.va/holy_father/john_paul_ii/letters/1979/documents/hf_jp-ii_let_19791129_bolla-francesco-ecologia_sp.html

———. 1981. *Human Work (Laborem Excercens)*. In *The Priority of Labor*, edited by Gregory Baum, 95–152. New York: Paulist Press.

———. 1987. *On Social Concern (Sollicitudo Rei Socialis)*. Boston, MA: St. Paul Books & Media.

———. 1991. *On the Hundredth Anniversary (Centesimus Annus)*. Washington, DC: United States Catholic Conference.

———. 1992. "Apostolic Constitution, Fidei Depositum, Publication of the Catechism of the Catholic Church." In Catholic Church 1992, pp. 1–7.

———. 1995. *The Gospel of Life (Evangelium Vitae)*. Boston, MA: Pauline Books & Media.

———. 1998. *Faith and Reason (Fides et Ratio)*. Boston, MA: St. Paul Books & Media.

Pope Leo XIII. 1882. *On St. Francis of Assisi (Auspicato Concessum)*. http://www.vatican.va/holy_father/leo_xiii/encyclicals/documents/hf_l-xiii_enc_17091882_auspicato-concessum_en.html

———. (1891) 2000. *On the Condition of the Working Classes (Rerum Novarum)*. Boston, MA: Pauline Books & Media.

Pope Paul VI. (1966) 1993. *Devoted Mother (Alma Parens)*. In Ingham & Shannon 1993, 101–109.

———. 1967. *Populorum Progressio*. http://www.vatican.va/holy_father/paul_vi/encyclicals/documents/hf_p-vi_enc_26031967_populorum_en.html

————. 1968. *Of Human Life (Humanae Vitae)*. Boston, MA: Pauline Books & Media.

————. 1971. *Octogesima Adveniens*. http://www.vatican.va/holy_father/paul_vi/apost_letters/documents/hf_p-vi_apl_19710514_octogesima-adveniens_en.html

Pope Pius XI. 1931. *Quadragesimo Anno*. http://www.vatican.va/holy_father/pius_xi/encyclicals/documents/hf_p-xi_enc_19310515_quadragesimo-anno_en.html

Stanton-Rich, Diane. 1987. *Becoming Peacemakers: An Introduction*. Elgin, IL: Brethren Press.

United States Conference of Catholic Bishops. 2001. *Global Climate Change: A Plea for Dialogue, Prudence, and the Common Good*. www.usccb.org.

Van Den Goorbergh, E. A., and T. H. Zweerman. 2000. *Light Shining through a Veil: On Saint Clare's Letters to Saint Agnes of Prague*. Bondgenotenlaan: Peeters Publishers.

————. 2001. *Respectfully Yours, Signed and Sealed, Francis of Assisi: Aspects of His Authorship and Focuses of His Spirituality*. Bonaventure, NY: Franciscan Institute.

————. 2007. *Saint Francis of Assisi: A Guide for Our Times, His Biblical Spirituality*. Bondgenotenlaan: Peeters Publishers.

Wadell, Paul J. *Happiness and the Christian Moral Life*. New York: Rowman & Littlefield.

Warren, Kathleen A. 2003. *Daring to Cross the Threshold: Francis of Assisi Encounters Sultan Malek al-Kamil*. Rochester, MN: Sisters of St. Francis.

Wolter, Allan B. (1988) 2003. "Scotus's Ethics." In *Scotus and Ockham: Selected Essays*. St. Bonaventure, NY: Franciscan Institute, 173–83.

Wolter, Allan B., and Blane O'Neill. 1993. *John Duns Scotus: Mary's Architect*. Quincy, IL: Franciscan Press.

Zagzebski, Linda. 1998. "The Virtues of God and the Foundations of Ethics," *Faith and Philosophy* 15: 538–53.